SEEDS of AWAKENING

SEEDS OF AWAKENING

Cultivating and Sustaining the Inner Life

Molly Vass-Lehman, Paula W. Jamison, Thomas Holmes, Gayl Walker
Paula W. Jamison, editor

*Holistic Health Care Program, College of Health and Human Services,
Western Michigan University, Kalamazoo, Michigan*

This book was funded by the Fetzer Institute, Kalamazoo, Michigan

Seeds of Awakening: Copyright 2001 by the Fetzer Institute.

Acknowledgement of permissions for the use of text and photographs can be found on pg. 230-31.

Book and cover designed by Gayl Walker

Please keep in mind that the recommendations made in this book are general guidelines and are not meant to replace formal medical or psychiatric treatment. Individuals with medical problems should consult with their physician or appropriate health care provider to discuss modification of activities described in these pages that are relevant to their unique circumstances and conditions.

This book was originally published in 2001 by New Issues Press, Western Michigan University (ISBN 1-90974-04-3 and ISBN 1-90974-05-1).

Reprinted in 2003

Published by
Holistic Health Care Program
College of Health and Human Services
Western Michigan University
1903 West Michigan Avenue
Kalamazoo, Michigan 49008-5212
e-mail: holistic_info@wmich.edu
www.wmich.edu/hhs/holistichealth

ISBN 0-9740625-0-2

To our many students, past and present, whose courage and sense of wonder have inspired us; and to our colleagues and friends, who have embarked on the journey toward wholeness.

Contents

Preface

What happens when we have a moment of realization about a new direction we wish to take in our lives? What supports us when we seek change or strive to find a healthy, sustainable balance in our increasingly busy schedules? Why is it so difficult, even when we understand the need to take care of ourselves, to act upon our good intentions?

Seeds of Awakening emerged from a series of continually evolving dialogues with students, colleagues, family, and friends about the mysteries of human health and behavior. In the pages that follow we explore how to develop mindfulness and other awareness practices to create effective support for the sort of lasting behavioral and lifestyle changes recognized for their role in preventing or alleviating many health problems. Our focus is not on specific types of lifestyle changes: many fine books offer a wealth of information on the subject, and new research continues to be published at a breakneck pace. Instead, our intention is to offer an introduction to some of the multiple ways of knowing that can, if we are able to attend to what we are experiencing, offer us important insights into both the state of our health and our most pressing needs.

How, then, do we relearn the almost forgotten art of listening within? By inner listening, or attunement, we mean more than chance reliance upon intuition, although it too is important. The ways discussed below offer sustained practice in paying attention to bodily and emotional as well as external cues. If we are able to find a trusted means of returning to and re-evaluating our intentions, we are less subject to the pull of the multiple distractions that so often derail our most noble ideas. Moreover, as we learn to heighten our awareness of what is being communicated by our bodies, for example, we may discover that what was once a deeply held belief about what is needed to support our health actually needs refining and adapting.

The practices of rest, contemplation, creative expression, relationship, and work discussed in this book are deeply rooted in the human experience. Some, such as mindfulness practice and contemplation, derive from ancient spiritual traditions. Others are more modern or have secular roots. They all are based on the same premise: viewed holistically, our lives encompass more than just physical, emotional, social, or even spiritual aspects. As dynamic, living beings, we move in and out of periods of rest and activity governed by rhythms not of our own making. The rush of modern life, with all of its high tech comforts, often obscures our need for quiet, reflection, or just being.

The practices here offer the chance to move into a deeper experience of these rhythms as well as the opportunity to attend to messages that often go unnoticed when we are always focused on external signals. Endowed with the power to nourish the whole person, they offer us sustenance for the spirit, as well as the mind and body. When we feel nourished and sustained, we interact with the world around us from a place of wholeness. Our responses inform our relationships and work, as well as our connection with nature.

How we tend the seeds of awakening that sprout in our lives reflects our own unique gifts and life histories. However, developing the habit of mindfulness is the key to many of the other practices described in this book. Mindfulness in this context does not require the systematic study of meditation, although persons drawn to this practice can find resources that will guide them further if they so desire. Mindfulness instead refers to the cultivation of a type of presence, in body, mind, and spirit, that then allows us to experience more completely our creativity and vitality in all aspects of our lives.

The result of a collaborative effort, the pages that follow have been informed by our individual and shared vision of how to cultivate and sustain the inner life. In addition, our reflections have been immeasurably enriched by the stories of students, colleagues, clients, and friends who have touched our lives. Some of these stories appear below, although names and certain details have been altered for the sake of privacy. It is our hope that these accounts will encourage readers to experience the healing potential of discovering and owning their unique stories, whether through reading, writing, or exploring the integrative practices offered throughout the book.

Acknowledgments

Our efforts to explore and describe a genuinely holistic process of learning and self-discovery would not have been possible without the generous support and guidance of the Fetzer Institute, known for its pioneering work in furthering research and education on the relationship between the body, mind, and spirit in health and healing. The Institute's impact on the field has been wide-ranging and has helped us all in our efforts as educators and researchers. For his leadership and support over the last decade, we would like to acknowledge Rob Lehman, President Emeritus of the Fetzer Institute. Dave Sluyter and Mickey Olivanti, also of the Fetzer Institute, have been most generous in helping us bring this project to fruition. We would also like to recognize Joel Elkes for his role in inspiring us to attempt to capture our fluid ideas and bring them into the form of a book, and Mark Nepo, for his generosity in granting us permission to quote his poetry, as well as for his creative guidance into new territory.

The touchstone for our individual and collective efforts in creating this book has been the Graduate Certificate Program in Holistic Health Care at Western Michigan University. We would like to express our deep appreciation for the encouragement that we have received from the past and present deans of the College of Health and Human Services at Western Michigan University, Bill Burian and Janet Pisaneschi. Without their ongoing support—and the faith in our work that it represents—we could not have embarked on this mission to create the program or had the good fortune of being as successful in our efforts.

Special thanks to Karen Horneffer-Ginter, Jenise Brown, Theresa Ziadie and Christy Honsberger, for their editorial assistance, enthusiasm, and creativity, to Frank R. Jamison, for his watchful eye. We appreciate the support of John Walker for his technical assistance. We are also indebted to K'Anna Burton, Diane Melvin, and Fritz MacDonald, whose personal journeys have illuminated and continue to enrich our own reflection. We would like to thank our colleague Edo Weits who has contributed immensely to the success of our holistic health program. Last, our profound gratitude to all of our students, past and present, who have inspired every one of us with their courage and commitment to live each day with greater compassion and awareness. They have embraced the notion that it is possible for the ordinary layperson to assume responsibility for his or her well-being with a readiness that is at once surprising and touching. They have been a constant source of encouragement for us all.

We also want to extend our gratitude to Tom Seiler, Linda Judy, and Julie Scrivener at New Issues Press, Western Michigan University for their valuable assistance and expertise.

CHAPTER 1

Introduction

Awakening

I have woken from the sleep of ages and I am not sure
if I am really seeing, or dreaming,
or simply astonished
walking toward sunrise
to have stumbled into the garden
where the stone was rolled from the tomb of longing.
                    David Whyte, *"Easter Morning in Wales"*

Do you remember a time in your life when you first began to see yourself and the world around you in a new way? What was it that caught your attention? What led you to this turning point? What is calling you now, and where are you going?

There is a story in the Bible of a man who was blind. When Jesus restored his sight, all he could proclaim was, "I can see, I can see." This story is relevant to all of our lives, as each of us has our own personal tale of awakening. Each of our stories is imbued with a sense of the miracle of seeing for the first time. Like a blind person whose sight has been restored, we realize that our whole world and our sense of balance have changed. Beauty is all around, and we soak it into the pores of our being like a sponge. Our sense of who we are and what matters to us expands and allows us to touch—and be touched by—the world around us in new ways.

Nature offers us many images of this process of opening. Consider the common milkweed, which grows wild in fields and along roadsides throughout North America. When the time is right, the pods crack open and burst forth, spreading their seeds on the wind. The genus milkweed (*asclepiadacaeae*) is named for Asclepius, the Greek god of medicine, and throughout the ages, this lowly plant was thought to have properties that helped people learn to love and nurture themselves.

Creation myths, common to most cultures, emphasize the experience of awakening. Poet Mark Nepo tells a Tahitian story about the beginning of the world that points to this moment of breaking through and entering another reality:

> For a long period Ta'aora dwelt in his shell (his crust). It was round like an egg and revolved in space in continuous darkness. There was no sun, no moon, no land, no mountain. But at last, Ta'aora was pressing against his shell, as he sat in close confinement, and it cracked and broke open . . . and the world began. This process repeated and, moving through shells within shells, Ta'aora tore them all apart to create the universe.

What calls us to awakening in our own life: seeing a painting, meeting a mentor, undergoing a religious experience, or discovering the wonders of nature? Or does it come through suffering a loss: a divorce; the death of a loved one; an illness; or losing a job? Whatever the circumstances of our own moment of awareness, it joins us with others in a common bond of human experience. Once touched by the grace of wakefulness, we are never the same.

Jacques Lusseyran tells a poignant story of awakening in his autobiography, *And There Was Light*. At the age of eight, Lusseyran was permanently blinded in an accident at his elementary school. He fell against the corner of his teacher's desk, and the blow pushed the glasses he was wearing into the tissue of his right eye, which had to be removed. His left eye was also damaged, causing him to lose the sight in that eye as well. The remarkable part of this story is how as a child Lusseyran was able to emerge from this experience and awaken to a deeper reality in himself and the world around him:

> I was aware of radiance emanating from a place I knew nothing about, a place which might as well have been outside me as within. But radiance was there, or, to put it more precisely, light. It was a fact, for light was there. I felt an incredible relief, and happiness so great it almost made me laugh. Confidence and gratitude came, as if a prayer had been answered. I found light and joy at the same moment, and can say without hesitation that from that time on light and joy have never been separated in my experience. I have had them or lost them together.

The freshness of perception wakes up every fiber of our being, just as the experience of a new love awakens us to a love of life. We begin to see color, hear sounds, feel the wind, and touch the earth in a new way. Nothing looks the same, as if our lens of perception had been wiped clean. A kaleidoscope opens before us, and new patterns and ways of seeing unfold. Author and Jungian counselor Helen Luke speaks of this process in our lives. Seeking to comprehend the meaning of an image from a dream, she makes this discovery:

> I suddenly knew I was looking at [the cloth] from the wrong angle and I gave the cloth in my hand a quarter turn clockwise. Immediately I saw a beautiful and coherent golden pattern . . . to be seen in all its beauty by those who would learn to make the "quarter turn."

Once touched by the grace of wakefulness, we are never the same.

Once we see things in a new way, our vision feels effortless and magical. It is difficult to contain our enthusiasm and the newfound energy unleashed in us. We want to share it with all around us and are often surprised when others cannot see things the same way that we do. What do we do with this precious experience? How do we commit our time and attention to the message that it holds about our own true nature and essence? How do we nurture the fruit of awareness in our lives so that it may ripen and be harvested to heal ourselves and ease the sufferings of the world?

CHAPTER 2

The Call

Hearing the Call

The language of the call to awakening comes to us from the wisdom traditions, with their emphasis on the cultivation of the subtleties of the life of the spirit, but it applies equally to the richness and complexity of a holistic approach to healing ourselves and others. Opening to a new level of awareness, as described in the preceding chapter, represents the birth of something new in our lives. When the call comes in the form of a major illness or the death of a relationship, or the discovery of a hidden talent, we may, with a little encouragement, be able to see its potential value in our lives.

At other times, even being able to acknowledge or value these shifts in our outlook may be extremely challenging. Feelings of restlessness or dissatisfaction, or a vague sense of longing for something unnamed, perhaps unnameable, are subtle indicators that are often easy to ignore yet may eventually escalate into a sense of crisis. In its more dramatic embodiments, it is possible to see the call as an invitation. Its quieter, and perhaps more prevalent, forms may gently encourage us to be still and listen, utilizing not just our intellect but our heart and physical senses in order to even know what we are experiencing.

Allowing ourselves to hear the call means doing what we can to be open to the transformations within. It means a willingness to be with the unknown, even though we live in a culture that values action and results—or at least clarity. It is no surprise that at times the temptation may be overpowering to *do something* the moment we sense that change is afoot. Yet what may be needed instead is to allow these faint whisperings to emerge more fully, giving our intellectual, emotional, and intuitive faculties the space and time to attend fully to the opportunity before us. Positioning ourselves so that we may truly hear demands more of us than a passive silence. It requires a readiness to listen, to engage in the process with all our senses. It requires a willingness to act when the time is ripe. It may mean tempering a burning need to know with patience, as we begin to sift and sort through information that—if we are able to attend to it—is coming to us from all directions.

Our awareness of the fragility of the call to awakening has grown out of our combined experience as educators and health care professionals. Over the last twenty years of teaching in the field of holistic health, we have come to realize that something has been missing in our attempts to help individuals sort through the constantly expanding deluge of often contradictory research available in the areas of health care and wellness. As a result, we have slowly shifted our focus from disseminating information about health to helping others learn to listen to our existing inner knowledge and cultivating a relationship with our bodies. The hallmarks of this relationship are care, listening, and trust. This

Nurturing this trust is essentially a process of coming home.

is not meant to deny or minimize the importance of understanding the effects of nutrition and lifestyle on diseases such as cancer, diabetes, allergies, and mental disorders, for example. Yet it is difficult to bring this knowledge to bear on our daily lives when we lack ways to understand and respond to our own needs in a supple and realistic way.

This view through a wider lens arose out of our understanding that although many people initially adopt new habits when presented with facts, statistics, and risk factors, over time they often return to their former, less healthy routines. On all levels—physical, emotional, social, or spiritual—lifelong patterns of behavior are difficult to relinquish. Even a seemingly simple change, such as giving up dairy products, may affect us emotionally by causing us to feel deprived of a favorite "comfort food." Or we may react with frustration and feel isolated when all of our co-workers order out for pizza at lunchtime. If we listen only to what others tell us, whether it is in the form of well-researched scientific studies or the latest diet update on the Internet, we remain all too vulnerable to the power of outside influences to distract us.

However, it is possible to open to change in a more multidimensional and balanced way. We can begin to value—as well as cultivate—many forms of awareness. Then we can more easily begin to listen to and develop trust in our bodies. The outcome is a sense of awe and newfound respect for what we hear, feel, and see. Nurturing this trust is essentially a process of coming home that enables us to tap into our inner wisdom in all its myriad forms. When we are in touch with this deep reservoir of knowing, we strengthen our capacity to respond authentically to the mass of often conflicting information coming to us from so many sources.

Reconnecting with the world of the physical senses is a crucial way of fostering a sense of curiosity and openness about ourselves and our need for change. Experiencing the world with the exquisite intensity of a child may bring us in touch with our wish to adopt more sensible eating habits or perhaps stimulate us to exercise our creative powers. In the following chapters we will explore this and other ways that help attune us to the forces of growth in our lives. Recapturing our most elemental relationship to the world through our senses goes hand-in-hand with a sense of wonderment, and the language of the body as we experience it on the deepest level offers us a sense of the miraculous as it opens us to new levels of awareness.

It is not enough simply to be receptive to new sources of wisdom, however. If we are truly to support the process of this call to awakening, we must be able to hear it in the first place. Holding ourselves in readiness for the call requires intention, in the fullest meaning of the word, while cultivating our capacity for discernment permits us to act—and not merely react—to what our senses tell us.

Holding ourselves in readiness for the call requires intention, in the fullest meaning of the word.

Recapturing Wonder

MOLLY VASS-LEHMAN

It is the children of the world who remind us of the need for wonder in our lives. Spiritual teachers of all faiths, such as Jesus and the Buddha, have encouraged us to look to children for teachings about the spiritual value of wonder. The capacity to look around us with awe is at the heart of healing and is the root of all true education. As Rob Lehman, President Emeritus of the Fetzer Institute suggests:

> Aristotle was perhaps the first of many to observe that true knowledge proceeds from wonder. [To] wonder is to stand in awe of the ultimate mystery of life and to understand that mystery exists not merely in the ecstatic but in ordinary daily life. Eliot Deutsch observed that wonder, unlike curiosity, does not try to figure out, to answer, or to explain. We do not wonder "at," "about," or "why"—we wonder "with."

Children bring this sense of awe and curiosity to many supposedly "ordinary" things. A woolly caterpillar becomes an opportunity to pause and watch in amazement. A snowstorm that worries or burdens us as adults is an exciting adventure, a magical event of whirling white beauty. Babies find unending fascination and delight in something as simple as playing with their own toes. Children see life as a series of countless marvels unfolding all around them.

When we open to the mystery of life, we experience grace.

Unfortunately, all too soon we lose our sense of the world as a place of wonder. Over the years, as expectations and demands increase, the weight of the world settles in upon our shoulders. Forgetting the incredible miracle of ordinary moments, we allow our capacity for astonishment to go to sleep. Occasionally we still experience fleeting glimpses of mystery, only once again to be pulled back into the preoccupations of our lives. We see a look of awe on someone's face and pause to remember something vital and familiar in ourselves. A light in someone's eyes, a look of amazement, have the power to touch us all. We see it in the faces of great spiritual teachers such as the Dalai Lama, who manifests a childlike quality wrapped in great wisdom and clarity. Wonder implies faith and trust in mystery, the unknowable, the unimagined.

Accepting the mystery makes it possible to live with a sense of peace and compassion. Any truly spiritual journey teaches humility as well, as we come to understand that we cannot know the reasons for much of what happens to us and our fellow beings. Life can bring us immense, unimaginable joy, or suffering of unbearable intensity. Yet these seemingly contradictory experiences are underlaid with a common thread. If we allow it, such powerful experiences stir in us a sense of awe that inspires us to let go into something larger, beyond ourselves. When we open to the mystery of life, we experience grace.

Even if our capacity for wonder has lain dormant for many years, we can consciously rekindle it. Slowly we can learn to turn our attention to the miracle of life inside and around us, noticing simple things: a bird's song or the angle of light as the sun sets. We learn to find the extraordinary in the ordinary. Everyday acts, such as walking and eating, can become a time to celebrate the wonder of our bodies and of nature. This growing awareness reminds us of the preciousness of all life, and we experience a profound sense of gratitude for what we often take for granted. The poet Mary Oliver beautifully evokes this sense of newly awakened awe in her poem, "The Summer Day":

> Who made the world?
> Who made the swan, and the black bear?
> Who made the grasshopper?
> This grasshopper, I mean —
> the one who has flung herself out of the grass,
> the one who is eating sugar out of my hand,
> who is moving her jaws back and forth instead of up and down —
> who is gazing around with her enormous and complicated eyes.
> Now she lifts her pale forearms and thoroughly washes her face.
> Now she snaps her wings open, and floats away.
> I don't know exactly what a prayer is.
> I do know how to pay attention, how to fall down
> into the grass, how to kneel down in the grass,
> how to be idle and blessed, how to stroll through the fields,
> which is what I have been doing all day.
> Tell me, what else should I have done?
> Doesn't everything die at last, and too soon?
> Tell me, what is it you plan to do
> with your one wild and precious life?

A poem like this helps us remember a way of being in the world where we can feel, touch, smell, and hear the life around us. Taking even a fleeting moment to pay attention to our surroundings as we walk from our car into work—noting the breeze on our skin or the sound of a child's voice—brings our senses back to life. When we open our awareness to the seemingly small things in life, we begin to discover that despite all our busyness and productivity, we have truly been asleep.

Integrative Practices

Touching the World

The human body is a miracle we often overlook. Consider our hands, for example. They are our most expressive appendages. They can caress, create, and communicate. We often use them as tools, as unmindful of their exquisiteness as we would be of a hammer or a pair of pliers.

For this practice, sit quietly with your hands on your thighs, palms down. Relax and breathe down into your belly. Feel your body relax. Draw attention to your hands. Focus on the intention to move your right hand. Breathe in and out several times as you pay attention to the experience of the intention to move this hand. Notice any subtle feelings. Then slowly lift your right hand straight up. Move slowly. Repeat this process with your left hand, first focusing on the intention to move, then moving the hand. Now hold both hands out in front of you with the palms down and take ten slow breaths. Pay close attention to the experience of your hands.

With your eyes closed, slowly move your hands close to each other without touching, palms facing, then back and forth slowly without touching for five or six breaths. Begin gradually increasing the speed of these movements and continue for about a minute. Stop when your hands are slightly apart. Let your hands sink gently back to rest on your thighs. Sit for a few minutes, being aware of the sensations in your hands, arms, and shoulders, as well as throughout your body.

Remembering Wonder

Take a few moments to relax and reflect on the times you

have felt wonder, awe, or amazement. Did you ever gaze in fascination at the color and pattern of a sunlit leaf, or watch snowflakes land on the sleeve of your coat? Or was there a favorite toy that captivated you with its scent or texture? What did it feel like to be moved by the look on a friend's face? In your mind's eye, go back to one of those moments. What did it feel like? Does wonder have a place in your life right now?

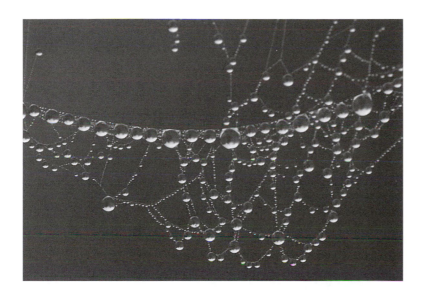

Recovery of the Senses

Molly Vass-Lehman

When we recover our sensory capacities, then, we look upon the world with wonder. Generally we think of our senses as doors to the external world, permitting us to experience our connection with the vast world outside of us. Yet our senses not only tell us about the outer world. They also tell us much about our deepest needs or longing for a new way of being. Indeed, our awareness that something is missing in our lives is often accompanied by the discovery that we have lost the ability to detect what we really need. At such times we know deep down that something somewhere can support us in the process of returning home. Yet we may not know what it is, or even if we do recognize it, we are unsure of how to bring it into our lives. Perhaps we misread the results of our well-intentioned efforts, as happened with one of our students.

A young woman by the name of Shannon had enrolled in a class on holistic health because she was looking for ways to improve her diet and patterns of exercise. She was anxious to make some of the lifestyle changes that she understood to have a role in disease prevention. By the second evening of class, she spoke openly of her growing recognition of her addiction to busyness, to keeping herself occupied. She also expressed her eagerness to learn and practice stress reduction techniques, especially the relaxation exercises and guided meditations offered at the beginning of class.

As the semester continued, however, Shannon began to arrive late, just as the periods of meditation were ending. The spark that she had originally brought with her seemed to have dimmed, yet she persisted with all the other assignments and exercises. One day, when there was a discussion about the meditations, she expressed her frustration at "not getting it." Each time she would attempt to meditate, she said, she fell asleep. Relief showed on her face when others described their struggles to stay alert. Perhaps she simply needed to sleep, a classmate proposed. Offended at first by what seemed to be a criticism of her level of self-discipline, Shannon reluctantly agreed to use the time she had set aside for meditation simply to rest.

For Shannon, accepting the validity of her body's message was a struggle at first, and recognizing her fatigue was frightening. Yet slowly her understanding and acceptance of her need for rest ripened, and over time she was able to deepen her capacity to attend to her true needs for nourishment. She discovered that at times something as simple as rest can bring us back into connection with the inner dialogue between our body and the world around us.

Understanding how we have become so distanced from our

bodies' messages can help us find a way to respect and value their importance. The demands and amusements of modern life separate us from nature and its rhythms. Instead of sitting around a fire on a winter's night, families watch television, often alone, in rooms scattered through houses lighted against the dark and heated against the cold. No longer is it common for us to sing songs together for amusement. Instead we have become spectators, listeners, and passive consumers of entertainment transmitted through an electronic process removed from the immediacy of the sensory experience it is meant to convey to us.

This shift has undermined our reliance upon immediate sensory experiences. Fewer and fewer among us use our hands and bodies to earn our daily bread. Instead, we often use our minds and increasingly sophisticated equipment in the workplace. Taking the time to be present in body, mind, and spirit as we walk across a freshly mown lawn has become a type of private luxury. Sensing the grass with our whole being—its textures and scents, the sensations of light, coolness, or dampness, perhaps even the hum and irritation of a mosquito—is an experience that is often drowned out by other urgencies in our lives or relegated to vacations. Even when we allow ourselves such moments, they are rare and quickly forgotten. In our collective lives, we do not honor them and find few ways to make time for them. Most importantly, they no longer provide us with a frame of reference for how we experience our bodies.

Our lack of attention to the spectrum of sensory experience accompanies a learned distrust of our senses conjoined with an ancient uneasiness about our physical nature. Throughout the world, cultural and religious traditions surround the human body with mysteries and taboos that reflect an intuitive understanding and awe of the power of our being. The legacy of a scientific tradition, in which the human senses are often presented as unreliable sources of information—fruitful as it has been in expand-

The demands and amusements of modern life separate us from nature and its rhythms.

ing our knowledge—has further eroded the value we give to our inner experience of the body.

Our mistrust of our bodies' messages is all the more profound when our capacity to sense has been injured by trauma or other challenging circumstances. These can occur very early in life, even in the womb. Such injuries are holistic, affecting all dimensions of our being—body, mind, and spirit. When this wounding occurs at a very early stage of development, we may quickly learn to compensate for our real needs for food, touch, or attention by other means, which fail to satisfy our actual hunger.

The noted Swiss psychotherapist J. Konrad Stettbacher offers important insights into how this process unfolds. He suggests that human beings begin life as "all body," and that our reactions are governed by our senses. Even while still in the womb, sensing gives rise to feeling, and we learn to strive for or avoid the pleasures and pains that we perceive:

> [the infant's] experiences and reactions, combined with what it senses and feels, already form an "opinion," or what I shall call its "inner attunement," about the nature of good and bad. This inner attunement created by the linking of our faculties of sensing and feeling is the foundation of the discriminating "I."

Stettbacher goes on to say that if something interferes with this process, the result may be a conditioned or patterned response that may remain with us throughout our lives.

This original reaction may have been effective in the primal situation, but it is not truly helpful or even appropriate at other times. Many examples can be found to illustrate this idea and how it plays out in adult life. For many of us, our mothers or fathers may not have been abusive or overtly neglectful. Yet they may also not have been physically or psychically present to meet our valid longing to be held, touched, or comforted.

Struggling within the limitations of the nuclear family, our parents may have been overwhelmed by their own needs or those

Slowing down to pay attention brings us into the timelessness of the present.

of our siblings. For example, a child's first expressions of the need to be held or touched might be met with anxiety or exhaustion from a mother who is also trying to meet the demands imposed by caring for three other children. In her hurry, she may give the child food to calm her down. Yet the child's real need is to be comforted and attended to in other ways. Then the child may try to seek other ways, such as rocking, to comfort and calm herself. She may begin to associate food with fulfilling the need, even though it does not. As she grows up, she may unconsciously continue these patterns and wonder why, at the age of forty, she reaches for chocolate chip cookies every time a twinge of loneliness, perhaps barely recognizable as such, comes over her.

It is possible to become so accustomed to denying our real needs that we do not even recognize when we are truly hungry...

It is possible to become so accustomed to denying our real needs that we do not even recognize when we are truly hungry for food or rest, or are called upon to attend to the body's other natural functions. Despite the advertisements all around us, feeling tired is not our body's way of telling us that we need another cup of coffee! Yet it is easy to see how this confusion could begin in early life. As children we had the capacity for sensation and deeply felt our needs, but conscious interpretation and understanding lay beyond our powers. Such confusion is hauntingly described in the book, *Sleeping with Bread:*

> During the bombing raids in World War II thousands of children were orphaned and left to starve. The fortunate ones were rescued and placed in refugee camps where they received food and good care, but many of these children who had lost so much could not sleep at night. They feared waking up to find themselves once again homeless and without food. Nothing seemed to reassure them. Finally someone hit upon the idea of giving each child a piece of bread to hold at bedtime. Holding their bread, these children could finally sleep in peace.

These children had experienced profound loss. Even when it was once again possible to meet their present needs, their deep insecurity about having enough in the future persisted. If children such as these, when they are old enough, cannot begin to understand the pattern of their longings in a conscious way, it can torment them throughout their lives. If, however, they can begin to recognize the source of their needs, they can be released from some of their fears for the future and from the past. They can begin, perhaps, to open to the present.

Instead of viewing our sensory abilities only as a link to the outer world, it is helpful to consider them as a doorway to the present. Life in a fast-paced society has dulled our senses, leading us to look constantly for the extraordinary, the sensational, or the spectacular. Yet it is still possible to learn to respond to the simplest and most ordinary things in life. We can learn to attend and observe, as one of our colleagues did when she was a child:

> I used to attend a church camp in Leland, Michigan. On Sundays, the camp director, who was also a spiritual director, would have us go into the woods, pick a square-foot plot of ground, and get to know it for an hour. I remember how at first I thought this was silly—what would I be able to see? How would I be able to look at it for an hour? Then I noticed a small insect climbing over the blades of grass. It crawled up and down, through and around each blade, and took almost an hour to travel one foot. I was fascinated.

If we are fortunate, when we were young someone may have shown us how to look closely and notice small details. But chances are, even if that was the case, we have grown up favoring one sense over the others, naturally preferring vision to hearing, or turning our attention outward or inward. Each of us is unique and relates to the world in her or his own fashion. However, whatever our previous habits or inclinations, a time often comes when it becomes necessary for us literally to experience the world in a new way. Slowing down to pay attention, whether by focusing on a previously overlooked detail in our surroundings or by fully allowing ourselves to feel the weight of our bodies as we sink into a chair, can take us out of our usual goal-oriented actions and bring us, however briefly, into the timelessness of the present. Consciously looking at the world from a different angle can arise from a choice to shift our focus, and doing so heightens our awareness of even the most mundane and repetitive acts.

Integrative Practices

As a result of our habit of regarding our senses as doorways to the world outside us, we seldom stop to think deeply about how our bodies can be affected by the light, sound, tastes, odors, and touches that constantly bombard us. Through the delicate, sensitive instruments known as our eyes comes much of our knowledge of the world around us. But our eyes serve us far more extensively than as mere cameras on the world. They are also receptors of light, which affects our well-being in profound ways. In the following situations, bring your attention to the light in your environment and how it makes you feel.

Seeing, Hearing

Choose a room in your house in which you feel particularly comfortable. Sit there for a few minutes and become aware of your experience of light in the room. What does the light feel like? Pay attention to the physical sensations that you are experiencing when you are in this place, as well as any emotional responses that may arise. How do you feel in the room once you are more aware of the light?

Now go to a place outdoors where you feel comfortable. What is the light like there? How does it make you feel?

The next time you go into your office or workplace, sit for a few minutes and become aware of your experience of the light in this place. How do you feel when you are there?

Now find a place, either at work, at home, or elsewhere, in which you are not comfortable. Be aware of the light in this environment. How does the light affect the way you feel in this place?

As you go about your business over the next week, be aware of the lighting in various stores, shopping malls, office buildings, or homes that you enter. How do you feel in these environments?

Sensory Experiences

The same experiment can be carried out by focusing on any of the other senses. This time, begin by paying attention to the sounds in a comfortable space at home, or the odors you encounter as you walk through your workplace. How do these sensory experiences make you feel? Notice any images or thoughts that arise during this practice.

The Body As Grace

MOLLY VASS-LEHMAN

As we begin to develop a sense of trust in the body's wisdom, we experience a feeling of wonder and gratitude. As the grandeur of the world around us inspires awe, so does the miracle within us that is the body. Working with many health care professionals and educators over the years, I have become aware that health education curricula for children and adults are primarily concerned with delivering information *about* our bodies, instead of providing opportunities to connect with the inner experience of living as a complex and dynamic organism.

Something so simple as being granted permission to truly acknowledge our "embodiedness," though it runs against the grain of much of our cultural heritage, could have an important impact on fostering healthy lifestyle changes. Even the word *embodied*, or the notion of relationship between "us" and "our bodies," suggests a division between body, mind, and spirit and carries with it an implied value judgment. A way of learning that invites us to acknowledge our wholeness would move to heal that split by helping us to begin at an early age to listen to and trust our inner experience and wisdom.

Indeed, many of us have learned to ignore our bodies' messages. When our childhood curiosity about our bodies and sensory experiences was met with suspicion or discomfort, we slowly turned away and stopped listening to our vast inner resources. We no longer heard the dialogue going on inside us. We learned to look to others to understand what was happening to our health, growing to mistrust or forgetting entirely our inner intuition and wisdom.

In the process, we have lost the habit of attending to what our body has to communicate. And the body, refusing to be silent, then speaks to us in other ways: through pain or addictions, or when we find that our appetites make us blind consumers of more and more things that stubbornly fail to satisfy our deepest needs. It is no wonder that addictions are rampant in our culture.

Some experts estimate that 90% of the American population is either chemically addicted, affected by the addictions of others, or suffers from compulsions. It is not surprising that one of the most prevalent mental health disorders in our society is anxiety, and that so many individuals seek external ways to reduce this chronic state through overworking, overconsuming, or through habits such as watching television. Yet addictions of any kind fail to bring us back into greater connection with our inner yearning or the message that it holds for a possible healing in our life. In fact, such behaviors often bring a greater sense of isolation.

Discovering that we can rely on our bodies for guidance can, over time, bring a sense of confidence to our ability to choose healthful ways of life. For years, people have asked me, "Why do

A way of learning that invites us to acknowledge our wholeness would help us to begin to listen to and trust our inner experience.

you eat health foods, and why are you a vegetarian?" My reply is not what it used to be. Before I would say that eating in this way decreases the risk of heart disease, cancer, and other illnesses, as well as using fewer of the world's precious resources. Now I reply that I eat this way because I feel much greater joy and peace when I eat well and care for my body. Health, healing, and joy are intimately connected. It is out of this experience of joy and wonder that we can begin to care for our bodies, feeling a sense of reverence and love.

When we love and feel gratitude for our bodies, we will be more likely to make choices to give ourselves healthy food, rest, and exercise. Instead of focusing on the sense of strangeness or even deprivation occasioned by a new eating style, we learn to use our senses to notice what this body is telling us. If we learn to listen to our hearts, lungs, and other organs, as to well as our backs, feet, hands, and other body parts, we will know what is necessary to support good health.

When we love and feel gratitude for our bodies, we will be more likely to make choices to give ourselves healthy food, rest, and exercise.

This practice of listening to our bodies does not eliminate the need to consult outer authorities. Indeed, the value of the "expert opinion" or the knowledge of others increases if we are able to anchor it in our direct experience. Then we are able to evaluate what we read or hear by attending to the wisdom grounded in the living processes of the body itself. When we rely solely on information obtained from others we bypass this source of wisdom. Thus disconnected from our deepest sense of values, we are left to seesaw between our rational minds and the range of emotions constellated each time we feel tired, fearful, or overwhelmed.

Even when we recognize this deep source of wisdom, however, it is a challenge to return to a deep connection with our bodies. It takes sustained, regular attention to overcome a lifetime of feeling a step away from our inner impulses and intuition. Only with time are we able to develop capacities to hear, feel, and sense at increasingly subtle levels.

We take so many of our blessings for granted, especially the extraordinary gift of health. We give time and attention to so many things in our lives that we often fail to care for our bodies. Then something—exhaustion or illness perhaps—reminds us to pay attention. Learning to listen to our bodies takes time and patience. When we develop a loving relationship with our bodies we come to honor a wisdom deep inside us. Thus, we are able to meet life from a place of trust in our own completeness.

Making this journey homeward requires re-imagining the very meaning of health.

Making this journey homeward requires re-imagining the very meaning of health. If we become focused on an idealized state of health or fitness, it is easy to forget that health is not an end in itself—it supports our abilities to accomplish our life goals. This is an important message, because even in the name of health and wellness we can ignore the body's signals as we push beyond our limits in the moment. Today many individuals suffer from overuse injuries related to exercise, while others override their nutritional needs by following the latest diet program.

In a culture that values speed, quick fixes, and cures it is difficult to slow down and listen as we move forward with any diet or exercise program. It takes time to cultivate the ability to hear the body's messages and to trust our intuition. It may even seem as if we are swimming against the tide of our health care system, which emphasizes quick solutions to health problems—a situation that often creates deeper issues in the long run. When we totally relegate our health to an outside authority we can lose a sense of connection to our own inner process and the sacredness of our bodies. By ignoring our instincts, we can actually do violence to our bodies in the name of health.

If, however, we are able to slow down, we may begin to watch ourselves, observing our bodies as a mother watches her newborn child. We can take the time to experiment, to see how we feel when we eat certain foods or try different exercises, actually noting the results. We can quit reading about our health and pause to look at and listen to what we see and feel in the moment. Then we could recover a sense of our natural rhythm and learn to trust our true nature. A line from a poem by Mark Nepo says it all: "Birds don't need ornithologists to tell them how to fly."

Integrative Practices

Sometimes we touch with the innate grace of our bodies. It is possible, however, to reconnect with this sense of underlying beauty and grace.

The Body As Grace

Find a comfortable position, with your head and spine straight, so that you can begin to breathe deeply. Feel your body begin to relax as you breathe fully into the belly, the center of your body. Now, as you settle into a place of relaxation begin to create a picture in your mind of yourself in full, radiant health. Imagine yourself full of grace and beauty. What do you look like? What do you feel like?

Continue to hold this picture of yourself in grace and beauty. At the same time, try to get a clear sensory feel of your body and your surroundings.

Imagine yourself going through the day feeling this way. How do you move, talk, and respond to your environment? What choices do you make when caring for your body? How do you feel in the morning? as the day goes on? in the evening? Now, imagine that the day is ending and you are getting ready to go to sleep. What do you feel like now?

Explore your feelings about this experience and the images that came to you.

Nourishing the Body and Soul

Food and water sustain our vitality and well-being. Every person requires a unique combination of foods to meet his or her individual needs. Learning to listen to what your body is calling for in the moment is part of the art of living well. Choosing life-giving nutrients for the body is a gift of care for this sacred vessel.

Reflect for a moment on what you know about the impact of nutrition on well-being. How often do you give your body the nourishment it truly needs? How does your body respond? Are there any changes you might make today?

Learning to Listen Within

MOLLY VASS-LEHMAN AND THOMAS HOLMES

If we are to honor the body's needs and our inward calling to move into a more balanced and compassionate relationship with ourselves, we must begin to determine what is truly important to us. Images from nature have been used to describe this process of sensing what is essential to our being. Among them is the sunflower. In the morning it turns and raises its head to the east. As the sun rises it follows its course across the sky to the west. When we quiet ourselves we too are able to sense the direction that our lives need to turn in order to receive the sunlight that will allow us to grow. However, this can be difficult. For in some ways we are like sunflowers in a parking lot, surrounded on all sides by artificial lights that distract our attention from the sun. The artificial lamps do not carry the full spectrum of light that we need in order to nourish our souls, and we become spindly, weak plants unable to turn toward the healing source of light.

How, then, do we go about recovering our ability to sense what we most need? What enables us to respond to our inner call instead of reacting to all the competing distractions that we face each day? Along with recovering our connection to our sensing selves, we must rediscover our ability to *discern* what is vital to our well-being.

Discernment is a term that refers to our capacity for discrimination—for sorting and setting apart—in the immediacy of the moment. All dimensions of experience are included: body, mind, and spirit. Wendy Wright captures the meaning of this process, once again evoking the image of the sunflower:

> Discernment is about discriminating: sifting through and evaluating the evidence of our focused attention. It is not, however, identical to problem solving. It is not simply a question of lining up the pros and cons concerning a particular decision we must make and then judging which choice is feasible, or determining which gains the most support or which will benefit us, or others, in the long run. Discernment is more like the turning of the sunflower to the sun.

This depiction implies a return to a natural, free process in our inner being. Once we allow ourselves to enter into this organic relatedness, we can see with clarity what is needed in the moment. We can know which direction holds the light. A deep inner attunement allows us to align ourselves with the external world in ways that are nourishing and life enhancing. Our true sensory capacities emerge as we learn to listen carefully to the wisdom within and respond to this inner guidance. Looking outside of ourselves for solutions may seem more efficient. However, while we may benefit from seeking the wisdom of others, such information is of limited use to us if we do not attend to our own experience.

An example of the importance of acknowledging the power

Along with recovering our connection to our sensing selves, we must rediscover our ability to discern what is vital to our well-being.

of our own experience is seen in a story that a colleague shared about his mother, Martha, who found out that she had stage four cancer of the colon and liver. At this stage such cancer is considered too advanced to be curable.

The surgeon who removed the tumors and her family thought that Martha should not have "palliative" chemotherapy, since in his experience it would actually diminish her quality of life. When she consulted with an oncologist, however, he convinced her and her family that a low level of chemotherapy would make her more comfortable and have none of the side effects that they had all heard about. Yet the side effects did occur. Martha soon began to experience the sore mouth, loss of hair, and diarrhea clearly associated with the chemotherapy. It was less clear to Martha and her family whether her fatigue, loss of ability to eat, and irritability were side effects or caused by the progressing cancer. How much worse would she be if she were not on chemotherapy?

Martha persisted with the treatment, trusting in the medical system, though her body was screaming to stop. She became depressed and began to lose interest in the life remaining to her. The oncologist responded by prescribing an antidepressant.

Three months into the treatment, while visiting with her son, she shared that when she had asked the oncologist how long the chemotherapy would continue he had told her at least another year. Martha said that it felt like a life sentence in prison.

At this point the voice within her rebelling against the treatment became so loud that it could no longer be denied. With the support of her family she discontinued the chemotherapy and began treatment at a holistic health center to heal from the effects of her treatment. Within weeks she began to regain her appetite and her energy, and was able to experience joy in life, sharing the time she had left with her family and friends. Her agitation and irritability yielded to peace and joy as she came back into harmony with her inner voice and heeded the cries of her body.

When we give ourselves over to the control of others, we sense that things are not right with our world and feel powerless to make a difference. We may lose interest in life as depression sets in. As time goes on, we become further disconnected from the inner cries that we are unable to voice. If we are able to wake up and muster the forces that allow us to listen inwardly, we can create a change that will allow these inner voices to have a place in guiding our lives. Then, if we are lucky, we will find support in our environment and can transform these inner cries into action.

Usually this process is not as dramatic as it was for Martha. Instead, more subtly, we may gradually lose touch with key aspects of ourselves, as we submit more and more to external expectations and demands. And because it is so easy to lose touch with the inner self, following through on the resolutions we make to change our behavior is difficult. At first, accustomed to overriding our fatigue or irritability, we forge ahead, unaware of the body's subtle internal signals until we lose patience with the whole enterprise and revert to the illusory comfort of past routines. Caught up in a socially sanctioned ideal of work habits, body type, or diet and exercise patterns, we model our behaviors on styles that have little relevance to our unique constitutions or life situations.

Relearning to listen, as the monastic traditions put it, "with the ear of the heart," takes time. It demands that we become reacquainted with ourselves during times of quiet and spaciousness, all too rare in our busy lives. One way to make room for such moments in an intentional, conscious way is to adopt regular periods of quiet, concentrated listening or watching in the form of any one of a variety of age-old contemplative practices. For if we continue to ignore our own inner wisdom, the gap between what we know about ourselves conceptually and our own experience grows ever larger. And our inability to live out these concepts in our daily lives becomes a source of frustration.

Many examples of the discrepancy between the conceptual

If we continue to ignore our own inner wisdom, the gap between what we know about ourselves conceptually and our own experience grows ever larger.

"ideal" and actual life experience are encountered in the domains of health and spirituality, where we articulate these ideas eloquently but neglect to embody them. We work for peace but find it a rarity in our inner lives. We speak of the value of relationship but have little time or attention for our mates and families. The burnout experienced by so many members of the helping professions attests not only to the incredible demands imposed by working surrounded by an endless stream of human misery, but also to our inability to remember—and reconnect with—those elements of everyday experience which can nourish and restore us. And tragically, this sense of disconnection only intensifies our numbness, as it did for a woman that we will call Joan.

Joan worked for years for an organization dedicated to the eradication of world hunger, traveling throughout the Third World trying to effect change in small communities and villages. Over the past year she had been to Africa and Asia several times, and had returned to the United States exhausted and overburdened. Suffering from a severe bacterial infection, she spent several months trying to regain her physical and mental health.

At home in Michigan, her work continued to haunt her. She felt responsible for many of the people she met during her travels, especially the women and children. She knew that many of them would die because of the lack of food and medicine. Ill and overwhelmed by a sense of powelessness, she fell into despair. It was months before Joan regained enough strength to function in a routine way, and even then she was plagued by feelings of ineptitude because of her inability to take care of the people she had visited. Years of constant effort to help relieve the suffering of others had left her emotionally drained and physically incapacitated.

Joan's story is that of many individuals who, setting out with good intentions and a sense of mission, forget that they too need care and nurturing. Taking the weight of the world upon her shoulders she pushed her body beyond a point it could handle. In doing so, she forgot her own needs for rest and inner replenishment.

If we are committed to listening to our inner needs and giving this new awareness a form in our everyday lives, we need to find a way to start. The act of letting go is a place to begin. Though it is difficult, the need to release some of our old ways is similar to a snake's need to shed its skin before it can grow. Slowly, feeling our way instead of adopting wholesale what we have read or heard from our friends, we learn to determine which aspects of our lives are no longer essential or even toxic. Unfortunately, no one can give us this knowledge. However, this capacity to discern between the living tissue of our lives and that which is no longer vital is a practice that is essential for making space for new life. At the same time, letting go does not imply that what we no longer need was useless or that we are condemning it in some way. Like a gardener, we turn over last year's habits and activities so that they may become part of the soil to feed this year's plants. This turning over of the old creates a space for and also nourishes that which is to come.

It can be difficult, even frightening, to part with something familiar to make space for the new and unknown. For Martha, discontinuing chemotherapy meant releasing the hope and trust that she had invested in the medical system. Letting go of a familiar source of authority was so difficult that the situation had to become very bleak before she would consider it. And to turn away from the known, she needed something else to turn to. She had to find an alternative that would incorporate the messages she was getting from her body and inner self and that at the same time could offer her hope and comfort. Even though we know it is time to release certain habits, we cling to them because they offer security.

The task of letting go can be made easier if we first bring our

Letting go does not imply that what we no longer need was useless or that we are condemning it in some way.

attention to those things that we know nourish us. Before we can pull the weeds from our garden we must first learn to recognize what we wish to cultivate, which seeds and plants we wish to nourish in the garden of our everyday life. Our experience of awakening provides us with a taste of the wholeness and fullness of life that we seek. This yearning for wholeness becomes a guide that tells us when we are moving in a direction that supports our deepest nature. Developing the capacity for awareness and attention furthers our responsiveness to this process.

The chapters that follow offer glimpses into some of the many ways we can support this process of sifting and sorting and letting go. Our task at these times is to slow down, open our senses, and become aware of the opportunities for breathing in spirit. As we do this we discover that what "inspires" us, or breathes spirit into our being, comes in many forms. Even more importantly, we begin to learn how it feels when we stand in a place of truth, this essential place in our being that many have called the soul, or the self.

Our experience of awakening provides us with a taste of the wholeness and fullness of life that we seek.

Integrative Practices

As we learn to listen more deeply within, we also discover what types of experiences best guide us and which ones have the most power to distract us.

Creating a Space for Listening

Allow time for yourself to quiet down from your usual activities. Finding a still posture, close your eyes and bring your breath down into the belly. For the next few minutes rest your awareness on the sensation of your belly as it rises and falls with the breath. As your body relaxes, begin by turning your attention to someone who is very dear to you. Feel the warmth and affection that you have for that person, not focusing on the person so much as upon the feelings that she or he inspires in you.

Shift your focus, then, to yourself, allowing the feelings of warm regard to remain. For the next few moments just be still with your breath, feeling what it is like to be regarded in a warm and nonjudgmental way. Breathe this feeling deep into your belly or imagine yourself sitting in the center of a sphere suffused with this warmth. Now ask yourself, What is it that I truly need?

Your answers may not come in words. Pay attention to the images, thoughts, or sensations that arise. Regarding yourself with the care you would give your dearest friend or child, take a few moments for reflection. Be aware of how you respond.

Inner Dialogues

One of the ways that we can come into a deeper awareness of what is important to us is to imagine ourselves in dialogue with another. Allow yourself some time to reflect on an area in your life that feels "out of kilter" to you—feeling overworked or unresponsive to the needs of a family member, for example. When you have a sense of what is troubling you, pick a time when you will be able to write while undisturbed. Write a dialogue between yourself and this "other." Allow each side to take turns. Some people find it is easiest to write dialogues of this sort as they would appear in a play, but the form is not important. This is a time to write quickly, whatever is in your head. Don't worry about consistency or creating a "character."

When you have run out of things to say, stop. Go back and read what the voices have said, paying careful attention to their comments. Has listening to them added to your insights about the situation in any way?

CHAPTER 3

Cultivating the Ground

Intention and Practice

PAULA W. JAMISON

Hearing the call is a far cry from heeding it. We have all had the experience of meeting or hearing about someone whose gifts to the world inspire us. The worldwide outpouring of grief at the death of Princess Diana a few years ago is a reflection of how many were touched by her life and her devotion to finding her own truth. It is impossible to know how many young people altered their career choices to devote energy to the causes she championed. The vast increases in money donated to the charities that she supported provides a more concrete indication of how people were drawn to honor someone they admired by contributing to the projects that she had chosen. Others among us may have been equally inspired by the life and work of such figures as Mother

Theresa, Martin Luther King, or Gandhi.

On a more personal level, perhaps we have taken a class or workshop and been startled by the delight of a new experience. Attending a yoga class, for example, may give us a new sense of calm and ease in our bodies, transforming the ache of moving long-neglected muscles into an experience of wonder. We may even practice daily, on our own, returning to the class each week like a sponge, ready to absorb each new posture or way of breathing. At the end of six or eight weeks, we find ourselves set loose, full of resolve to continue this new practice, only to discover to our dismay that the time we set aside for yoga is gradually gobbled up by other activities. Or we come down with the flu or strain our backs or just drift away, intentions forgotten. We judge ourselves harshly because we think we can never "stick with it."

Adopting new activities and then gradually discarding them is common in a world that presents us with so many choices. Such trial and error is an important part of the exploration necessary when a person is discovering hitherto unfamiliar ways of being. But it is also emblematic of a more complex issue. How often do we experience a sense of new direction in our lives and then lose sight of it completely? How often do we look around us for inspiration, only to find ourselves caught up in judging our deficiencies and, in effect, stifling the new voice within? How do we remember the call and allow it the necessary space and time to take root in the ground of our being?

The sections of this chapter each address a different way of cultivating the often fragile first stirrings of awareness. Something as simple as the act of paying attention has great power to shift our sense of ourselves and thereby change our world. Opening to the surrender offered by true rest, or discovering new habits of being in our daily rhythms by viewing them through the perspective of mindfulness and ritual or as distilled by regular journaling are ways to support and sustain our process of awakening. Such

Something as simple as the act of paying attention has great power to shift our sense of ourselves and thereby change our world.

practices are helpful not only because they guide our intentions to remain true to what calls us. They also contain the potential for creating a sense of spaciousness. They have the capacity to ground us in the present moment and suspend our nagging pre-occupations with a past we cannot change and a future we cannot control.

Each of these practices is a discipline, not in the narrow sense of a harsh punishment or grinding routine but, seen more broadly, as a form of devotion. In today's language we have a better understanding of the term when we think of its cognate, "disciple," a word whose root evokes the notion of a pupil or student. Disciplines, then, are teachings, paths of learning. These ways or paths are also referred to as "practices": the focus here is not on doing something over and over again until we do it "right" or "perfectly." Here practice simply means *doing* and suggests the notion of repetition. Doing again and again we bring into form what began as intention.

Over time, as we devote our energies to one or more of these practices, we can slowly learn to develop trust in the powers of our inner as well as our outer senses. We are able to bring previously hidden dimensions of ourselves into form. As we bring the fruits grown from the seeds of our awakening into our relationships with ourselves and others, we continue to work the ground that supports us, growing more and more attuned to our true nature and that of others.

Viewed holistically, our lives unfold as a dynamic process, which is only imperfectly summed up by our attempts to name and analyze it. In other words, each of the approaches outlined in this chapter complements and somewhat overlaps the others. Each of them, in a slightly different way, offers opportunities to fine tune our awareness of what we and others are saying, just as each offers a different view of the enactment or expression of what we are experiencing. Different people, then, will be drawn to adopt different practices. Some of these disciplines may be more challenging or less inviting than others. Discovering a practice that we can hold, not rigidly or obsessively but to which we can return with enough regularity that it begins to inform our vision of who we are, nurtures and sustains a sense of commitment to our lifelong process.

Contemplation

MOLLY VASS-LEHMAN

One of the most fundamental ways of supporting the call to awakening is to slow down and listen, to allow ourselves the time to absorb and relate to our inner as well as outer experiences. The notion of contemplation provides a lens that helps us understand and value this process. Whether as a formal spiritual practice (developed in most of the world's religions) or as an intimate part of the simplest activities of everyday life, contemplation allows us to bear witness to the mystery that is present at all times, should we choose to attend to it.

It is important that we distinguish between contemplation in a general sense and contemplation as it refers to deep states of meditation or prayer. Both have value and serve us in different ways. Both are founded upon our willingness to cultivate inner stillness and openness, which make it possible for us to experience the sacred. Each of us is different, however, and to practice the habit of contemplation we each must find our own way of "looking attentively and thoughtfully." This contemplative outlook does not result in extraordinary experiences. Instead, it creates a heightened awareness of the beauty and wholeness in our daily lives and relationships. Understood in this way, contemplation encompasses the fullness of human experience, including the joy and suffering that are a part of the order of life.

Contemplation is not the domain of certain individuals only, or of any one spiritual tradition or set of practices. Moments of insight or transformation can come in the most unexpected places and situations. We cannot be attached to the need for the perfect environment, complete silence, wonderful weather, or a place without interruptions. All of these conditions may help support us in contemplation, but in becoming attached to such conditions we may be caught by surprise. The trick is to let go of our expectations and allow experiences to come in their own time and place. If we are to live out of our own true nature, we must let this voice make itself known.

Whether we are devoted to gardening or to Buddhist practices, the purpose of contemplation is the same: to lead us to the heart of compassion. Contemplative practices include gazing on nature, washing dishes, or sitting in formal meditation. Each form can help us learn to quiet down, to listen, and to observe. Places of beauty and solitude can give us a break from the routine, noise, and bustle of daily life, yet there are many times when we find moments of great peace and insight while in the midst of noise and the mundane.

Even in the most appalling of human conditions—the starvation and cruelty of war, the physical and psychological torture of a prison camp—there are inspiring stories of individuals who

Contemplation encompasses the fullness of human experience, including the joy and suffering that are a part of the order of life.

have found the center of their being, the stillness within. Natan Sharansky's book, *Fear No Evil*, offers an example of this extraordinary ability to sustain—and be sustained by—contemplation under dire conditions. The author, a Jewish dissident, describes the ordeal of his nine years of imprisonment in the Soviet gulag. He was systematically stripped of everything that he cherished—family, possessions, and his freedom.

The one thing he was allowed to keep during his custody was a pocket-sized book of psalms given to him by his wife as he was being arrested. Several times during his confinement the prison guards would take the psalm book, and each time Sharansky would go on a hunger strike until it was returned. Some of these hunger strikes went on for periods of one hundred days or more. The practice of reciting the psalms offered him a way to transcend the deprivations of his imprisonment. These times of contemplation were a doorway to freedom and enabled him to define the core of his being.

Contemplation, then, is an attitude toward life, not just an idea or practice. In this way, it can occur in any place or situation. There are many ways to support a contemplative attitude in our hearts so that we carry it with us wherever we are and in whatever we do. For example, we may go on retreat, a period of respite lasting for a day, a week, or even a month during which we set aside our usual preoccupations. During this time we are able to sleep, pray, meditate, write in our journals, read, walk in nature, carry water or chop wood, sing or dance, or just be alone. Such a period of intensive attention brings us into deeper awareness of the rhythms hidden below our normal busyness.

Helpful as these times are, however, if we cannot find a way to shift gears back into the habitual world without losing touch with the calm we found, we may begin to wonder about the point of contemplation.

Many individuals speak of their yearning to cultivate contemplative practices in daily life. Some live alone, and others have families. Some have full-time work and immense responsibilities, while others lead less demanding lives. Despite these different lifestyles, contemplative practice can enhance the quality of each one. An attitude of contemplation helps us to see the quiet beauty that is all around us in the world, in the faces of the people in our lives or the way a cat stretches, as well as in the mundane tasks that take up so much of our time. We can begin to cultivate what the monastic traditions have called the "listening heart." This contemplative way of seeing, hearing, and feeling brings richness and depth of meaning to our lives. It allows us to know what is real and essential. It helps us move toward freedom and wholeness as we see more clearly into the truth of the moment.

We can look to a number of guides to help us cultivate a greater capacity for contemplation. Coming into such stillness enables us to view life through a broader lens of love and compassion, to see all the ways that we are called to serve in the world. Being able to look at ourselves and our world with a contemplative eye allows us to regain something long lost, buried under the details of everyday life. It does not have to be an elaborate process. Fostering a contemplative attitude can be as simple as remembering our need for times of rest.

Integrative Practices

The notion of contemplation extends our capacity for inner listening to all of our interactions with the world—living and non-living around us.

Coming into stillness enables us to view life through a broader lens of love and compassion,

Paying Attention

Spend some time sitting quietly in a location of your choice, outside or inside. Close your eyes and listen carefully to the sounds around you. Then shift your attention and listen to the sound and rhythm of your breath and heartbeat. Note any feelings, thoughts, or images that arise.

At another time repeat this activity by focusing on a different sense: by paying attention to what you see, touch, smell, or taste.

Being Present, Doing Nothing

Set aside a time when you will be undisturbed.

Now, in silence just be in this environment, without music or reading, or writing. Simply observe your surroundings, trying to experience this place as if for the first time. Notice how you feel—are you relaxed, or do you feel bored or anxious?

If your mind begins wandering or you begin to make "to do" lists, turn the focus of your attention inward, on the sensations of your breath or of your body as you sit or stand. What are your reactions to this time of quiet?

Remembering Rest

MOLLY VASS-LEHMAN

We are a weary society, over-functioning in all aspects of our lives. Work, relationships—even leisure and the service we provide—can become a source of pressure and exhaustion. Many of us have lost the ability to rest. We seem to be moving at such a speed that we feel as if we are out of breath trying to keep up. Is it any wonder that diseases such as chronic fatigue syndrome are on the rise? It is easy for us to get caught up in the assumption, so prevalent in our society of round-the-clock work shifts and stores that are open twenty-four hours a day, that we can simply overlook rest or that sleeping a few hours is the same as resting. Culturally, we gauge our worthiness by our capacity to produce. Rest, by its very nature, seems to produce nothing. We may even disparage rest, just as we so often complain about the long nights of winter that in earlier times slowed us down and turned us inward.

Nevertheless, many of us seek rest. Yet we do not remember how to find it. We look for ways to fit it into our lives, treating it as if it could be relegated to the compartment where we store all the other beneficial habits and practices we long to adopt. Leisure activities and disciplines such as meditation or yoga may help us remain in touch with the experience of rest, but these practices often create yet another demand on our already over-committed day. In all our striving, we have forgotten one crucial point: rest does not involve doing. We cannot practice rest. It is not a discipline with a specific form or structure. We do not have to close our eyes, sit in the lotus position, and count breaths—even though such practices may help along the way. Rest seems too simple a concept to get our attention. It cannot be packaged in audio or videotape programs. Despite its great importance in our lives, our culture undervalues rest.

Truly, we have lost the meaning of the word "rest." It is not merely the absence of being busy. It is not a willful effort, a planned experience, or a scheduled activity. Rest is a state of mind, an opening into our inner lives, a process of unfolding and allowing. Rest offers us a lens that makes it possible for us to perceive everything in our lives with greater definition, giving us the opportunity to relate to the world in a fresh way.

The essence of rest is best understood through the characteristics associated with it. Rest depends on qualities of safety and comfort. These feelings imply that we are able to experience trust on a deep inner level. The inward place of rest is undemanding, open, gentle, soft, merciful, and kind. We seem to sink into rest, even surrender to it. We let go of effort and struggle. Rest is different from laziness or sloth, though, because when we are at rest our state of mind is unburdened and unclouded. Rest is clarifying, refreshing, like a cool stream of water or a breeze.

Rest seems too simple a concept to get our attention.

Rest returns us to an inner rhythm and affirms our intuitive wisdom. It reassures us that we have a way of knowing what we need, when we need it, and that no one outside of ourselves can give us this information. True rest gives us the inner space we need to listen carefully to our bodies, minds, and spirits.

When we rest, time seems to stand still. Lost to the world as we are in that moment, we learn that it can go on without us. We come to recognize that we are "a speck of dust in the winds of time." Paradoxically, what accompanies this feeling of insignificance is a sense of belonging—we feel we are part of a larger web of creation, never in isolation. Rest brings us the understanding that there is unity in all things. This recognition is also fostered by the teachings of many of the great spiritual traditions. Thus it is no wonder that many religions refer to rest as an important part of the path to wisdom or awareness of the divine.

For example, Christians speak of the rest that brings us out of our isolation as "rest in God," a phrase that evokes the nearness of the holy, or sacred. Such insight arises when we are able to just let things be. The tradition of the Sabbath in the Judeo-Christian world, based on the biblical story of creation, allows for one day of rest each week. A practice known as Centering Prayer, with roots in the Christian monastic traditions, is becoming a popular form of contemplation that brings about this experience of deep peace and rest.

The prayerful nature of rest is conveyed by the Greek word, *hesychia*, which refers to the process of resting the heart in prayer. Such prayers come forth from a deep resting state, a stillness out of which the words are born. The Buddhist tradition, with its emphasis on living in the here-and-now, refers to resting in the experience of the moment. In this sense, resting means being at peace with whatever is happening now, acknowledging the richness of each moment. This experience can change our perception of time, slowing down our compulsion for busyness. Resting calmly in the now enhances our sensual capacities of sight, sound, taste, smell, and touch.

The process of opening the heart can be aided when we encourage our senses to rest. Throughout history, all major religious traditions have used fasting—a rest from food—as a way of heightening spiritual sensitivity. Periods of abstinence from food are often accompanied by silence, a rest from speaking that is also communicated by the ancient meaning of "fasting": it originates in a Hebrew word that means "to shut one's mouth." Seen from this perspective, the deeper meaning of fasting is to rest the body and mind so that spiritual capacities may be enhanced.

Recovering the practice of rest in our lives is important preparation for illness and death. Rest teaches us the value of patience and timing, and how to honor the cycles and seasons of our life. It helps us hold ourselves and others gently in times of fragility and transition. Jack Kornfield, a writer on Buddhist spirituality, recounts the following story from *Zorba the Greek*, as a poignant example of the necessity for cultivating equanimity and patience in our daily lives.

> I remembered one morning when I discovered a cocoon in the bark of a tree just as the butterfly was making a hole in its case and preparing to come out. I waited awhile, but it was too long appearing and I was impatient. I bent over it and breathed on it to warm it. I warmed it as quickly as I could and the miracle began to happen before my eyes, faster than life. The case opened, the butterfly started slowly crawling out and I shall never forget my horror when I saw how its wings were folded back and crumpled; the wretched butterfly tried with its whole trembling body to unfold them. Bending over it, I tried to help it with my breath. In vain. It needed to be hatched out patiently and the unfolding of the wings needed to be a gradual process in the sun. Now it was too late. My breath had forced the butterfly to appear, all crumpled, before its time. It struggled desperately and, a few seconds later, died in the palm of my hand.

Rest returns us to an inner rhythm and affirms our intuitive wisdom.

When we remember the meaning of rest, we can return inwardly to this place of repose and wait patiently for life to unfold around us. We can experience deeply both the miracle and sorrow of life, and learn to hold these experiences with love and mercy. This mercy is not born out of a sense of obligation or guilt, nor does it resemble "feeling sorry" for anyone or anything. The mercy we show ourselves and our lives at such times is more akin to the sense of the Hebrew word for mercy, the root of which means "womb." True rest is like being held in the womb. If we could rest more in each other's arms, hold each other more, our relationships could help heal us and the world. To touch and be touched can be restful. To hold a baby or pet a puppy can be restful.

Allowing ourselves to rest often brings a sense of gratitude for the blessings in our lives. It restores and heals our perspective. This is why it is important to recover rest, to honor it as part of the fullness of our lives. There must be a time for activity and responsibility, but it is also necessary to have time for digestion and gestation. We need a time to integrate, to savor the moments of our daily lives. This savoring process is essential, for it adds a sense of timelessness and spaciousness to our lives. Slowly biting into an apple while sitting in a grove of maples on a clear, crisp fall day can create a memory that may nourish us throughout a lifetime. The same apple, eaten on the run, in a rush from one meeting to the next, is forgotten in an instant. It neither satisfies physical hunger nor the longing for authentic connection with that moment in our lives.

All of us have memories of rest deeply embedded in our bodies and minds. I often recall that on hot summer nights when I was a child, my mother would tickle my back for hours until I fell asleep. Even today I can feel the lingering sensation of peace that accompanied those times, and this remembrance of the physical and emotional experience of rest is helpful during times of stress. For if we can remember what rest feels like, instead of merely acknowledging its value as an abstract idea, we have something to which we can return to help us restore our balance. When we permit ourselves to recall the actual experience of rest, we are more able to honor the natural impulse to step back and let things be.

If we cannot remember, if we think only of our need for rest, it becomes yet another obligation, something on our endlessly expanding "to do" list—and a source of stress. If we cannot enter into the experience of true rest, then we will continue to live our lives filled with unease and a deep-seated restlessness. Anxiety will continue to plague us, and we will keep making futile attempts to deal with it by medicating ourselves or trying to quench our thirst for peace with alcohol, food, or other addictive substances and habits.

While we are prone to forget it, rest is an essential part of the rhythm of life and central to our capacity for wholeness. Fortunately, we can start on the path of remembering rest at any time. For some of us, it is a long journey home to memories of peace and tranquility. Yet the mind, body, and spirit have amazing recuperative powers, and the experience of rest can be regained, once we begin to honor its place in the rhythms of our lives.

If everyone in our society began to rest more, would we be less productive? It is unlikely. In fact, being at home with rest would make us more patient, tolerant, and less violent to ourselves and others. No longer so tightly bound to the compulsion to keep moving and producing at all costs, we would have time to listen—to others as well as to our own hearts. Becoming more open to others leads to a greater sense of interconnectedness, which would give rise to greater compassion—not just for others but for ourselves. A world where rest was honored would allow us to experience our relationship to the world more fully. Rest is like the arms of creation around us, holding us gently and lovingly.

Trusting in ourselves and the world enough to rest, we offer

Rest is like the arms of creation around us, holding us gently and lovingly.

ourselves the gift of healing. As we come to experience true rest, we grow in our responsiveness, refining the gift of awareness of ourselves as well as others. This ability to attend to our inner and outer environments, which emerges from the soil of rest and contemplation, can be further nourished by the daily practice of mindfulness. As rest allows us to slow the pace of our lives, mindfulness makes it possible for us to truly be present and further cultivate the gifts of awareness and attention.

Integrative Practices

One way to become attuned to rest is to create conditions in which the body and mind let go of the tensions and bustle of our usual activities. Understanding and consciously choosing to honor our need for rest aids us in providing these conditions.

Resting Pose

The ancient practices of yoga include a number of resting poses, which are designed to allow the body to be still without falling into sleep. As noted yoga teacher and physical therapist Judith Lasater explains, these postures afford deep relaxation that is not possible during sleep, when our bodies are engaged in cellular repair and move about in response to certain necessary sleep cycles. A simple version of the pose commonly known as the "Tranquillity Pose" requires a blanket, hand towel, and a pillow. A timer with a quiet bell (or placed in a cupboard to muffle the sound) is needed as well. If you have one, a small cloth eyebag filled with grain is also helpful.

Set the timer for five to ten minutes. If you wear contact lenses you may wish to remove them. Lie flat on your back on a carpeted floor, in a quiet room with low lighting. Place the pillow under your knees to avoid stress on your lower back. The hand towel can be rolled lengthwise and placed under the nape of the neck for support. Since the body cools as it relaxes, cover yourself with the blanket. Close your eyes (the eyebag will provide gentle pressure on the eyes and shut out the light, but is optional). Allow your body to sink into the floor, as you allow your breath to become deep and slow. Remain in this posture until the time is up. When you leave the posture, do so by first rolling gently onto your side, gradually becoming more alert. Only then open your eyes and gently resume a seated position. Take a few more moments to come back into the room. Notice how you feel when you get up and resume your activities.

Experiencing Rest

How do you experience rest throughout your daily life? Keep a log for a week to ten days, noting when you feel most tired and when you are the most rested.

What does rest feel like for you? When is it difficult for you to rest? What habits or situations seem most conducive to rest for you?

Mindfulness

Thomas Holmes

One of the defining experiences of our era is the feeling that we do not have enough time. We rush from one thing to the next, trying to keep up with all that needs to be done. The range of tasks and the amount of information we are managing is ever increasing, and labor-saving technology only seems to expand what we have to deal with. We are all becoming "wired" to huge information networks—the answering machine, the cell phone, e-mail, and the World Wide Web—all of which only add to the pre-existing jumble of newspapers, radio, and TV inundating us with thirty-second sound bites designed to tantalize and keep our attention. Many of us have become so accustomed to this level of input that when we walk into a quiet house or get into our cars we turn on the radio to avoid the unfamiliar silence. We are so busy "managing" our very "full" lives that we forget to live.

One of the most powerful ways to resume living is to practice mindfulness. Mindfulness is the conscious act of bringing our attention to what we are doing or experiencing. Instead of being buffeted from one activity to the next or automatically filling each moment with the radio, TV, or a phone call, we practice drawing our attention to the activity at hand and being fully present with it. Through this act of bringing awareness to the present moment, and our experience of it, we begin to feel a sense of ease, calm, and peace. By expanding our awareness of ourselves in the here-and-now, we become more fully alive.

The practice of mindfulness is also a way to bring the contemplative spirit into everyday life. Being mindful does not mean that we will find "enlightenment" in some esoteric state. Instead it is a way to help us awaken into our every action and thought, thereby bringing the qualities of this awakened state—calm, peace, compassion, and joy—into the everyday world.

We can only experience life in the present moment. There is no other option. We can think of the past or the future, but this awareness of other times is an aspect of our present mind. Yet even though life can only be experienced right now, we usually get so lost in our "busy days" that before we know it, they slip by with ever-increasing rapidity. Always rushing to get to the next thing, we forget to enjoy the beauty of the people we love, the trees we drive by, the color of the sky, the taste of the food we eat.

This automatic living, where we do not pay attention, is the forgetfulness referred to in the great religious teachings, such as Buddhism. According to tradition, the Buddha defined himself not as a god or a prince but simply as one who is "awake." Being "awake" is remembering to bring awareness to the experience of our lives so that we can see the beauty of a child entranced with an autumn leaf, the peacefulness of the moon on a clear evening,

We can only experience life in the present moment.

or the miracle of our own bodies as we move about during the day.

This call to wakefulness can come in a number of forms. Sometimes we are jolted out of our forgetfulness by the sudden loss of someone close to us or by undergoing our own life crisis. In such moments we are again reminded of life's impermanence and the importance of savoring each moment. A number of years ago I experienced such a shock to my customary way of being.

On my birthday, as I entered my fortieth year, I underwent a risky surgery on my cervical spine. This procedure required approaching the spine through the front of my neck. The doctors had told me that without the surgery there was a fifty-fifty chance that I would lose the use of my right arm. They also mentioned that there was a one-in-one-thousand chance that the surgery would result in the loss of my voice. These odds seemed to make it an easy decision—until I woke up from the surgery and found that I had no voice.

As I reflected on my life as a psychotherapist, teacher, and administrator, I had the sudden wish that I had given up my right arm, for it was hard for me to imagine my life without the capacity to speak. In our everyday lives, how many of us sense the beauty and wonder of our ability to talk, to connect with others through this miraculous process called speech?

By chance, at the time of my surgery my wife was reading a book about an Irish boy who had cerebral palsy, and she took the risk of giving it to me to read. This boy's physical problems were such that he had been totally unable to communicate with the world around him.

Finally a dedicated teacher discovered that the boy could type using a pencil attached to his head. He had to peck out each word, but for him being able to make contact with others in this way was a great miracle. As I looked at my body from this perspective, I saw the wonder of the resources still left to me. I could see, hear, walk, write, smile. The horror at the loss of my voice gave way to gratefulness for all the capacities that I still had.

As it turned out, the loss of my voice was only temporary. After a month I was able to communicate in a whisper. After two months I could speak softly, and with rehabilitation my voice came back to normal. This is perhaps the greatest of blessings: to lose something very precious, to come to value during that time what you still possess, and then to have what you lost returned.

Being so close to losing something precious that we have always taken for granted is a dramatic but potentially painful way to discover its value. While we cannot avoid life's sorrows, we can learn to awaken to the gifts offered to us by the present moment. One of the miracles of mindfulness is that it can help us to feel grateful for what we have without first losing it.

So one aspect of mindfulness is being able to enjoy life as it is now. An additional benefit of mindfulness is that as we focus our attention on our immediate experience, a number of transformations take place in our consciousness. When we enter into the present moment, we begin to relax, to feel centered and calm. Often a quiet joy begins to emerge. As we become accustomed to practicing mindfulness, this deep and abiding sense of peace begins to inform our dealings with others and how we choose to pay attention to the things around us. When we practice mindfulness, we discover our potential to be awake and fully alive.

Bringing mindfulness into our lives does not require exotic techniques or ask us to adopt a rigorous schedule of meditative practices. Mindfulness begins with paying attention to what we are doing right here and right now. Instructions at the end of this section provide a way to begin, focusing on how to be mindful of breathing and such ordinary, every day activities as eating and washing dishes. We can bring this quality of simple awareness

One of the miracles of mindfulness is that it can help us to feel grateful for what we have without first losing it.

and attention to any other activity as well. The possibilities for mindfulness practice are unlimited.

Mindful living means that we no longer go through our lives on automatic pilot, a way of being that leaves us feeling out of control and tense. Mindfulness frees us to enter the present moment fully. When we allow ourselves to be truly present in our everyday lives, we discover that we are open to the beauty and miracle of life. Mindfulness also provides us with a deep sense of being centered. When we come to know, through our own experience, that we can truly return to the fullness of the present moment, a new level of trust may arise, one that allows us to move through the turmoils of everyday life while remaining awake and true to ourselves. We are able to carry out the simplest of actions with a renewed sense of presence. When we do so, we find that the most boring and mundane of tasks are transformed into rituals whose beauty and power nourish us and deepen our gratitude for the gifts that life has to offer.

Mindfulness begins with paying attention to what we are doing right here and right now.

Integrative Practices

When we live mindfully, we focus our awareness on the present moment. We pay attention. It could be said that mindfulness is a particularly acute way to contemplate the world around us; it also offers us a way to approach even the tiniest of actions, as the following practices illustrate.

Mindfulness of Breathing

Stop for a moment and become aware of your breath. A good

way to do this is to place your hand on your belly and notice how it rises as you breathe in and falls as you breathe out. Bringing our awareness to the sensations of the body in this fashion is a powerful way to return to the present moment. Bringing our attention to the breath allows us to focus on one of the most immediate experiences of living, the exchange of life-giving air with the world in which we live.

If most of your breathing seems to be located in the chest, it will be especially helpful to focus for the next few moments on letting your breath gently move the belly. You will gradually grow accustomed to this "belly breathing." As you do so, bring your attention to the sensations of breathing itself, of the air moving in and out through your nose. Allow your attention to rest gently on the sensations of this essential life process.

What did you observe as you turned your attention to the breath? Generally, as we begin to be comfortable with this process, we notice ourselves calming down and feeling a little more at ease. Returning our attention to the breath is a basic practice that is available to us at any time or place. If you work with this practice over a period of time, you will find that by simply returning your attention to the breath you have a means of calming and centering yourself in the midst of a busy life. As you become accustomed to returning to the breath in this way, it is possible to attain ever deeper experiences of relaxation and well-being.

Mindfulness of Eating

We can bring the same kind of attention to other activities as well. Eating is a good example. Approached with mindfulness, our meals offer repeated opportunities to awaken to the beauty of life. To introduce yourself to this practice, take a piece of your favorite fruit and bring your full attention to preparing it for eating. Be aware of how this fruit contains the sun, the rain, the soil, and the work of the farmer—all the elements that helped it come into being and arrive at your table. As you place the fruit in your mouth, allow your full attention to dwell on the taste, smell, and texture of the fruit. Each time you chew, savor the flavors that are released as the fruit gradually dissolves, as it is prepared for disgestion and then to become part of your being.

This attitude of mindfulness can be brought to other activities as well, such as dishwashing or meal preparation. It is best to start with tasks that you enjoy and that allow you to expand that joy. As you begin to have success you can then work with transforming your normal daily activities, which often are not enjoyable, into opportunities to touch the beauty of everyday life. This is returning to yourself.

Ritual

Paula W. Jamison

Ritual is as old as human experience itself and offers an important gateway to contemplative experience. It has been said that rituals are prayers in action, for when carried out with mindfulness and heart, rituals are the literal *embodiment* of the wish to be in the presence of something greater than ourselves. Normally we associate ritual with religious practice, such as the Jewish Seder at Passover, or the breaking of bread and sharing of wine in the form of the Christian Eucharist. Or we view ritual as one of the underpinnings of social life, employed to recognize and celebrate important markers on the human journey, such as birthdays, weddings, or funerals. But in truth our lives are shot through with ritual. We need only think of the way in which a parent, tucking her child into bed, repeats the same comforting story night after night to ease the young one into sleep. Thus rituals can be "great" or "small"; they come down to us from tradition or they emerge from our own creative energies.

Ritual has the power to allow us to enter sacred time and space. Whether implicit or explicit, there is an element of ceremony to ritual, and a sense of repetition as well. If we are able to attune ourselves to it, ritual offers us a feeling that we are taking part in something that is much greater than the events going on before our eyes. Inexplicably, we feel that we are part of something that has happened countless times, to countless others. Or, like the child who insists that a favorite story be told just the right way each time, we are drawn to a world where events follow one upon the other in a secure and stable order, allowing us to focus not on "what happens next" (for we already know that) but on *how* and *why* and *who*. When we participate in ritual we come to feel—on all levels of our being—that our lives are a part of the pattern of life itself. We discover that we are not alone in our joy or suffering.

When we participate in ritual we come to feel— on all levels of our being— that our lives are a part of the pattern of life itself.

Rituals also serve as social bonds that shore up group identity. "Why is this night different from every other night?" asks the head of the household each year to open the Passover Seder. To practicing and secular Jews alike, these words set the stage for recovering a sense of shared history, linking Jews from all over the world to the ancient story of the Hebrew exodus from Egypt. Celebrating the memory of this shared history establishes a common identity for all involved. Participants in such a ritual acknowledge their link to a common past, even as each individual has his or her own unique reactions to the actual celebration.

Ritual also allows us to see our connections with traditions and lifeways that have otherwise disappeared from the modern world. And because it is so laden with personal as well as collective memory, people attentive to the needs of their inner lives may find themselves struggling against the power of traditional ritual. For such a person, critically examining what was previously automatically accepted may be a crucial step toward developing a vision of what it means to be whole or healed from past abuse. At these times of inner growth and change, family rituals may become a burden, attending church services difficult, or once-enjoyed reunions with friends a source of stress.

Yet abandoning ritual often leaves us with a sense of loss. We may feel cut off from something we are unable to name, even as we attempt to set old memories and patterns behind us. At such times, or when ritual loses its meaning and no longer speaks to us, we may suffer, often unaware of why our lives seem cluttered yet empty of anything that nourishes the spirit.

For these reasons, we may discover that we wish to remain in touch with the expansiveness that ritual can bring us. To do so we may have to find a conscious way to enter into the ritual experience that is meaningful to us. Nourishing the vital connection that ritual offers can be an important part of a journey toward greater awareness and self-understanding. One way of doing this is through the creation of personal rituals. Taking care to create and maintain a small shrine on a shelf in the dining room or to say a heartfelt prayer before meals can bring us into a deeper understanding of the day's events and provide an important sense of connection to the world around us. For someone who is especially busy caring for others, taking a few minutes during the day to light a candle or contemplate a meaningful object offers an opportunity for regular recognition that busyness is not all that life has to offer.

In times of crisis or great change, our need for ritual may be especially acute, even though we may be least able to recognize it. Beth was in her forties when her husband suddenly left her. Money was tight, and she found herself struggling to raise two teenaged sons who were having problems in school and with the law. While she had a job that she loved and felt comfortable with, Beth was overwhelmed by the changes in her life. She was chronically exhausted. In addition to her children, two cats, a hamster, and a large dog, Beth had several rabbits that lived in a hutch next to the garage.

Burdened with taking care of everyone and everything, Beth thought seriously about finding homes for all the animals except the cats. Yet she began to notice that her twice-daily trips out to feed and water the rabbits offered her a sense of quiet that she had not anticipated.

She discovered that she was able to just *be* when she was out there with the animals, and what she had once considered a chore began to be enjoyable. She began to realize that she had always enjoyed caring for the animals but had never allowed herself to value that part of her life. As time went on, she found herself setting aside a few extra minutes for petting and handling the rabbits. Taking care of these creatures, she said, was like taking care of something small, unprotected, and wild inside her.

In the beginning, Beth would not have referred to what she was doing as a ritual. Later she began to speak of her special time with the animals and how it kept her in touch with a world that was far away from that of the law firm where she worked. Beth was, in effect, operating out of a kind of healing instinct, one that allowed her to derive nourishment from a part of her daily routine that she had previously overlooked.

Rituals can be deliberately devised as well. Setting aside a few moments each day for prayer or reflection can nurture the spirit. This experience can become even more engraved in our nature if we enter and leave it in a "special" way, one that clearly allows us to experience the transition from "ordinary life" with our bodies and our senses. Lighting a candle, playing soft music that is saved for only such moments, or taking three calming breaths before we begin makes it possible for the body-mind to shift out of its usual workaday mode. Within the "sacred space" of the ritual, we can be as simple or elaborate as we wish, keeping in mind that part of the power of any ritual is the energy that we give to it.

Rituals are crucial to any healing process. Even though we may take it for granted and chafe at its impersonality, conventional medical practice is full of ritual: we are made to answer certain questions, must sit in a waiting room before being escorted (usually) to a small cubicle in which we have to remove most or all of our street clothes and wear a special gown; we may fast or eat special foods; and we address the physician by a special title. Yet "these modern healing rituals often fail to honor deep human feelings, our need for sacred connection, and the ultimate power of the conscious mind."

We can help compensate for this lack of warmth by first understanding the ritualistic qualities of conventional medical practices and then by using the power of our minds to create healing rituals that can offer comfort and even boost our immune system.

Ways of working with ritual for healing purposes have been documented in a fine book called *Rituals of Healing: Using Imagery for Health and Wellness*. Here the authors offer suggestions for eliciting the body's responses to imagery in order to support physical as well as emotional healing. Working with images, requires focus and concentration. It forces us to let go of our rational mind's need to be constantly commenting and explaining. As a type of meditation, it allows us to enter the emotional and sensory experiences that accompany our imaginings and has positive results in boosting the immune system and in creating a sense of calm and ease.

Whether we are facing surgery or chemotherapy or dealing with powerful emotions, we can learn to open ourselves to im-

The boredom of the familiar, if we value it and listen to it, has much to teach us.

ages that have the potential to heal. We can do much to facilitate this imaging process by consciously making it into a ritual, in which we gently guide our bodies, senses, and our minds to do the needed work.

Healing rituals can take many other forms. Designed to provide a safe and calm haven for the spirit, they include special meetings with others undergoing a similar experience. Support groups, the most famous of which may be Alcoholics Anonymous, or more informal meetings create a special place and time in which people feel permitted to reveal themselves more fully than they can at home or at work. The bonds that emerge among individuals aware of their common suffering can create a powerful healing force no matter what the outcome of the disease or condition may be.

When a special time apart for sharing with others is appropriate, its effect is enhanced by paying attention to opening and closing the experience. Some groups use silent meditation, prayer, or hugs. During the time together it is possible to establish a rhythm that differs from the usual pattern found in social or business meetings. For example, one ancient Native American way of allowing all to speak from the heart derives from the use of the "Talking Stick." Participants are seated in a circle. A stick is passed in silence to one of the participants, who is given the time to speak from the heart about his or her own issues. Others must listen and refrain from comment until the stick is passed to them. Such a practice, during which time speech is surrounded by silence, allows each participant to tune in to the words of others as well as to what is happening in his or her own heart. Shared silence as well as shared speech is a way of moving into communion with others.

When we make or participate in ritual, we acknowledge our choice to act as well as to listen with our hearts to our experience. In so doing, we set in motion our body-mind's capacity to

Ritual has the power to allow us to enter sacred time and space.

heal itself. As we come to understand our experience of the rituals we have consciously chosen, we begin to see possibilities for treating other repetitious aspects of our lives with greater respect. The boredom of the familiar, if we value it and listen to it, has much to teach us. Just as the breath or a candle or a flower may be an object of meditation during formal practice, then, brushing a child's hair—with all the wriggling or arguing, all the affection and frustration either person may be experiencing—becomes a specific object of attention.

Once we choose to regard any activity as a ritual, we make an unspoken agreement to be with the experience, whatever form it takes. This is a tacit promise to hold it as valuable and to honor it, being as present as possible. And when the activity is over, we let go of the experience and leave the "special time" or "sacred space" and resume another level of activity. Thus the act of entering and leaving sets the ritual apart from other activities and makes it possible to isolate it as an object of attention.

The ceremony associated with such rituals is not found in externals but in the attitude that we bring to it. Indeed, we may wish to keep our sense of ritual private at times, especially if we are living with others who feel resistant or threatened by any perceived changes in our attitudes or outlook. Ceremony, instead, is a matter of dignity and respect, and it is up to us to determine how we can best express these in the space and time allotted to the task. For example, Japanese culture has elevated the tea ceremony to high art. For someone living alone who usually eats dinner while watching television, this expression of respect (for oneself as well as for the act of eating) may take the form of eating dinner at the table, in silence. For another, it may involve choosing to have flowers on the table, while others might choose to see the time spent eating and watching television as valuable in itself and decide to take a few seconds to pay attention to how they feel before changing channels. Taking turns watching favorite programs may itself become a family ritual.

Ritual offers us a particular vantage point that is useful when we attempt to integrate the practice of mindfulness into daily life. Our sense of ritual enables us to approach our individual, isolated human experiences as part and parcel of a larger pattern, shared by our fellow beings and echoing down throughout history. When we acknowledge our ability to choose or shape the rituals that fill our lives, we recognize new ways in which we have the power to mold our experience and walk our unique paths with dignity and courage.

Integrative Practices

Creating Ritual

We are usually most aware of ritual during holidays or as a way to mark major transitions, but ritual can add an important dimension to life at other times, too. Often we focus so much on the externals—gifts, the setting, creating a "perfect" atmosphere— that we lose sight of the real reason for ritual, honoring our deep connection with ourselves or others.

Take a few moments to settle into a state of relaxation, simply experiencing the ebb and flow of the breath. Turn your attention to an aspect of your life that you wish to experience in a more healing way through ritual. For example, if you do not already have a regular time of quiet, how could you lovingly create a space for yourself, even if it is just for five or ten minutes?

How would you enter this space, and leave it? In a simple ways, how could you shape this time? Over the next week, try enacting this ritual.

Discovering Ritual

Describe an experience of ritual that is or has been meaning-ful to you. What are the qualities of this time or activity that attract you?

How do you respond when a favorite ritual is changed? Have you ever chosen to adapt a familiar ritual or begin a new one? Do your favorite rituals include others or are they private?

CHAPTER 4

Seeds of Creativity

Expression and Healing

PAULA W. JAMISON AND GAYL WALKER

Many of us, if we think back long enough and hard enough to when we were children, can recall moments of total, utter exuberance, a feeling that we were bursting with the need to jump, to dance, to sing or shout for joy. There was a power in that energy, and a delight. Those impulses, not yet shaped or formed, were manifestations of our creativity, our need to *express* or bring out what lay inside. Creativity is a power within us. Whether it is perceived as disruptive (as adults often see it in children), frightening (with its potential to reveal the unknown), or undisciplined (not yet molded into a form that we can recognize or admire), our creativity is also a source of healing and deep abiding joy. The spontaneous creativity we experienced as children had an openness to it that we now often long for as adults. As children we scribble or draw for hours on end, make up stories, or try on our parents' shoes and pretend we are adults. For a time at least, we feel at one with the universe, lost in play, not yet locked into our separateness from the world of objects and animals.

And yet at some point, play turns into competition. As our efforts are judged by teachers and schoolmates we may begin to get the message that we are simply not "as good as" someone else at what we are doing. Along with this comes the accompanying thought that if we are not as good at this as other people, we should not be doing it. We may feel that we will not be loved or even liked if we do or make things that are not the best. We may secretly tell ourselves that we are not "talented" or "creative" because we are not "good enough" to make a living—or to create a product others would buy—with our abilities.

The messages we receive from others have a great impact on how we perceive our own abilities. For example, Sharon who had enrolled in an expressive arts course, stated that she was uncomfortable drawing or painting. She explained to us that when she was a child, her sister was "the talented one." This idea was conveyed not just in words but deed. For Christmas one year, her sister received a paint set with a rainbow of colors and many brushes, while Sharon was given a simple eight-color watercolor package. Hesitant at first, Sharon began experimenting with some of the activities in class. One day while at work, she left her journal of drawings open on her desk. A co-worker noticed it and casually remarked to her, "Oh, I didn't know you were an artist." Sharon reported that this chance comment opened her up to a new sense of possibility—she could draw or paint and be an artist for herself.

One manifestation of the call to awakening may take the form of a desire to express ourselves in new, unfamiliar ways. Like Sharon, we may find ourselves drawn to taking an art class,

Our creativity is . . .
a source of healing and
deep abiding joy.

or wanting to learn to throw pots. Or we may not be attracted to any particular artistic form, but feel restless and want to rearrange our furniture or plant a few tomatoes. It is not surprising that the need to reclaim our creativity often becomes pressing as we become aware of something stirring in our lives. At times such as these, we strive to align our inner vision, our authentic sense of who we are, with the outer world of people, objects, and work. We are drawn to bring our emerging inner sense into *form.* Perhaps it is a carefully laid plan, the discovery of previously unrecognized or stifled parts of our nature, or a new way of relating to others. In any case, we are driven to manifest the invisible, chaotic yearnings of our hearts and minds in the world of space and time.

Most of us associate creativity with the arts or with the discovery or development of a new technology or scientific breakthrough. As a result we often feel that we are not up to the task of influencing the world at large with our insights or talents. Yet creativity, and with it the urge to express ourselves, is given to each one of us, and it manifests in ways unique to each individual. What is creativity but our capacity to adapt to an unpredictable variety of circumstances, or to see and communicate the beauty of the world around us to others?

Our creativity comes forth each time that we joyfully or reluctantly attempt to find meaning in our lives, whether in the face of unbearable suffering, the mystery of a new life, or the monotony of the daily grind. We tap our creativity when we figure out how to streamline a procedure at work, come up with a joke to cheer up a friend or loved one, or modify a recipe. Creativity enables us to respond to life, both in our outer actions and in our mental and emotional core. Furthermore, the satisfaction that we crave from the process of being creative (what we are asking it to do for us) seems to be rooted in our need to recognize—and many times literally to see, hear, smell, taste, or touch—

our own "take" on the world around us.

If we ignore the stirrings within, either by minimizing their importance or saying that we are not up to the task of bringing them to light, we neglect a fundamental aspect of our humanity. At the same time, we close ourselves off to avenues of healing and to restoring a sense of wholeness to our lives. When we are unable to respond to our murky urges toward self-expression, the creative spark cannot be ignited. We have closed it off to life-giving contact with the world around us.

Answering the call to awakening means embarking on a journey to an unknown place. No matter how we are drawn to support this call, our journey cannot proceed if we do not muster all our resources, including those we may have undervalued or even thought that we lacked. The following sections focus on some of the more traditional areas, or media, of creative expression: language, the visual arts, music and sound, and movement. Each of these can lead us into a new sense of connection with ourselves. By touching our senses and our mind in these different ways, they can shift our vision. For people who engage with the world primarily through words, for example, learning to trust their ability to *see* may be an adventure into a new country. These excursions into new territory can free us up to look at our lives in a new light. They can help us learn to trust our resourcefulness as well as foster our awareness of the beauty all around us.

As we come to honor our innate capacity to see the world anew, we learn additional ways to support our unique ways of knowing and being on this earth. By granting ourselves permission to take the risk of allowing the unknown to emerge, we begin to see and hear what we need to know to continue on our journey. We may even discover that within us lives an artist whose strength and wisdom we had not foreseen, an artist who has much to offer if we are open to receiving these gifts.

What is creativity but our capacity to adapt to an unpredictable variety of circumstances, or to see and communicate the beauty of the world around us to others?

Languages of Healing

PAULA W. JAMISON

Language is a mystery, its origins shrouded in the mists of time. It is the medium through which our innermost being takes shape as we develop from infancy—the word "infant" literally means "incapable of speech"—into the ever-widening spoken realms of childhood, and on to adulthood. An overriding mark of our humanness, language reveals and conceals, opens avenues to truth even as it weaves webs of deceit. We have all experienced how the right word, uttered at the right time and with the right intent, can soothe or heal—or how a chance remark can forever alter a relationship or cause us to re-examine the very purpose of our lives.

Language plays a powerful but incompletely understood role

in the healing process. Recently, researchers and creative writers alike have begun to devote attention to the effects of writing on health and healing. Journaling, poetry, and storytelling are now recognized for their positive effect on the management of chronic diseases such as asthma. The roles of narrative and wordplay in some forms of psychotherapy have long been acknowledged. Like other expressive forms, language offers us access to our elemental capacities for imaging and feeling, which play an important role in our body's immune system. At the same time, as the instrument of rational thought, language also can take us away from the intuitive, into a conceptual world that separates us from the experience of body and psyche.

As we begin to explore new ways of being, we instinctively seek out a new language.

With its power to name, language brings order and control to experience. Language enables us to tap into primordial images and bring them, however awkwardly and imperfectly, into the world of time and space that we share with others. We communicate discoveries about the physical world, what plants to eat, where the game have gone, or the best route to town now that the bridge is out. Not that any of this is an easy task. The most concrete directions require precision, while conveying abstract ideas, sharing a dream, profound emotion, or spiritual experience may tax the teller's abilities to the utmost.

As we begin to explore new ways of being, we instinctively seek out a new language. We may recall times when we encountered a word used in such a way that it perfectly described a feeling or situation that we were experiencing: "Oh, that's what that is!" we would say, feeling a surge of relief that what had formerly been only a vague sense about ourselves now has a recognizable and culturally described form. Thus language fosters awareness of our experiences, especially when they take such shadowy forms as unease, fatigue, restlessness, or dissatisfaction. Until we name them, in a way we are their prisoners, for we lack the means to step away and behold them. We also lack the means to share our inner lives with others, or even the faint reassurance that what we feel is part of the realm of known—and named— human experience.

One way in which people come to a deeper understanding of the impact of words on their lives occurs when they are introduced to the notion of self-talk. An omnipresent inner monologue, our self-talk forms a constant low hum of commentary and response that we normally tune out. Yet anyone with insomnia or beset with worry knows how insistent a chatterbox the mind can be, and how difficult it is to find inner quiet by attempting to silence the ongoing commentary. Even so, we tend to dismiss our inner speech or associate it with unusual conditions or mental illness.

Giving this aspect of our inner experience a name opens our field of awareness and offers a way to pay attention to a generally neglected aspect of our lives. Then we may discover that we are constantly nattering on about something or other. With a little direction, it becomes possible to notice the kinds of things that one says to oneself, and how seldom one is kind rather than hurtful, at ease instead of anxious, accepting and not judgmental. Moreover, the inner monologue favors certain choices of expression. Becoming aware of how we talk to ourselves is useful in addressing how we behave toward others, just as it helps us understand how we may subtly perpetuate our own sense of isolation or inadequacy.

For example, we may have adopted the habit of speaking to ourselves in ways that would be totally unacceptable coming from someone else. "Oh, what an idiot!" Sue mutters to herself as she fumbles for her car keys. "Can't you do anything right?" Or someone struggling with anxiety begins to realize that her habitual response to any new situation literally takes the form of hearing, "You'll never be able to do that!" We all have our "favorite" habitual lines of this sort, and discovering that we are so hard on ourselves may in fact prompt us at first to fall into the very patterns of impatience or anger that we hope our newfound awareness will cure. Yet as with any mindfulness practice, consciously making an effort to hear ourselves with nonjudgmental attention pays off over time. Instead of tuning out what we do not wish to hear, it may be helpful to return to the breath exercise described in the section on mindfulness and spend a few moments relaxing the body.

In addition to helping us evoke and understand our inner lives, our words can create or erode a sense of community. This sense of where and how we fit in is heightened and elaborated by story. From the dawn of language itself, it seems, people have told stories. Whether ancient myths or the endless themes and variations served up each night on television, stories continue to surround us and are so omnipresent that we often lose sight of the power that they hold over us. Story is part of the cultural air that we breathe, and to live deprived of story—if this is even possible—would be to live an impoverished life indeed. Where does this human urge to tell come from? Why do we continually, almost obsessively, create story? To comfort ourselves? To arrive at some understanding—partial, literal, or symbolic—of our place in the world or how this mysterious and very big universe works?

We take the stories that we live by for granted and may not even recognize that they exist. Then something happens in our lives—perhaps a series of relationships that all turn out the same way, or a mounting frustration, or repeated failure in our work. Laying claim to our "story" may come through working with a therapist or counselor, reading a book, or overhearing a remark. In any case, once we begin to see our lives as a tapestry of interwoven stories, we have at our disposal an important way of bringing meaning to our lives and, if warranted, change. Sometimes this shift in perspective happens quite by accident.

When I was a child, one of my brothers made a seemingly trivial remark that altered my perceptions, although it took me

Once we begin to see our lives as a tapestry of interwoven stories, we have at our disposal an important way of bringing meaning to our lives.

years to realize its full weight. He was about nine years old and had come home from a rotten day at school, when the teacher was crabby and my brother had dropped his homework in a mud puddle. The child had a wonderful sense of humor, and as he was conjuring up an image of the class ogre who made off with his prize cat's-eye marble during recess, I burst out laughing. He began to laugh too—reluctantly, at first. But then he said, "This will be a funny story when I get bigger." The whole family adopted his line, which became our motto when things were difficult.

My brother's story, and the comment that went with it, became part of family lore because it offered a way to put a difficult moment into perspective. We could all tacitly agree that there would be another time when this did not hurt so much. Especially when things were not so funny, the notion that the sweetness or bitterness of the present moment could be shaped into a story with a life of its own was a reminder of the power of imagination within us all. Likewise we can choose to tell our stories, perhaps in the privacy of a journal, as a path to self-discovery or as a way to better understand those who are close to us. For example, telling the story of one's partner or mother can bring new insights and compassion to the relationship.

Paying attention to our stories can be a vital part of coming to understand who we are, what we want, and where we belong in this world. We ignore the importance of story at our peril, for then the stories we live are imposed on us by others. When we allow others to do all of the imagining for us, when we constantly turn to the television or mindlessly pick up a magazine, we let our own deepest stories lie fallow and unheard. Without realizing it, we adopt stories about who we are and how we should be (thin and young, for example) and what we should want.

Sometimes the longing to express ourselves has no relation to narrative, with the linking of events, or cause and effect. We may be drawn to poetry or to composing songs, or to jotting down a few short paragraphs—this is how I am right now, this is the world as I see it. If we are able to be open to what is emerging and not impose our pre-established ideas about what we want, we can allow the form to emerge from the writing. When we allow our hands, hearts, and minds to work, our writing will reveal to us what it wants to become. At such times we can literally attend the birth of something new and perhaps as yet unnamed.

We are all inheritors of language, and when we are able to relate to it with a child's awe and playfulness we are on the way to finding an important avenue to healing ourselves. By writing in our journals or simply using our gift of speech, we may discover the storyteller or poet within us and tap into a deep feeling of well-being and community arising from our ability to give voice to our part in the human chorus. Language also gives us the chance to revel in our playfulness—some people have an incredible gift for puns, nonsense rhymes, and jokes, or enlivening a gathering with a funny story or turn of phrase. Glorying in the sounds and meanings of words teaches us to notice subtle distinctions and attend to what we hear and even to what has been left unsaid. And sometimes, as we follow the magic of a story that makes something out of thin air, we notice a subtle stillness. Then, stopped in our tracks, we turn our awareness not just to language but to the value of silence.

Integrative Practices

Language has the power to open our awareness and help us lay claim to the stories we carry within us.

Safe Haven

After completing the following imagery exercise, it may be helpful to write about it, to make the place you have experienced more familiar and accessible to you when you need it. Begin by taking a few breaths, allowing yourself to experience the sensations of breathing. Allow your body to become soft and relaxed. Now let your imagination take you to a peaceful time or place where you found healing or felt especially safe. Perhaps it is simply a favorite comfy chair in your living room or a treehouse where you spent time as a child. Maybe this safe spot lies in your imagination—is it someplace in nature, where you are surrounded by beauty yet feel protected? In your mind's eye, become familiar with this place—what does the air feel like on your skin? What colors do you notice? what odors?

When you are ready, describe this place in your journal. When you have finished, set the piece aside, to return to it at another time. Hold the memories of being in this place within you, knowing that you can always return to it if you need to.

First Words

Cast your thoughts back to the people who cared for you when you were a child. Was there someone whose voice or way of speaking you particularly remember? What was that voice like—can you describe it? Do you recall any words or phrases that remind you of that person?

Were there any stories in your family about your first words? your first sentence? If you don't have an answer to that question, imagine what you first tried to say as a child learning to speak. What are your feelings toward that child, looking back?

On Keeping a Journal

PAULA W. JAMISON

One way in which we support the process of awakening is to keep a journal. If cultivated as a regular habit, journaling provides an opportunity to record—and thereby relive and re-examine—key moments and events. Practiced consistently, journaling can offer the chance to go more deeply into our responses before they are crowded out by the demands of our everyday routines. In this way we are able to bring to light what has disturbed or delighted us and honor it with our attention.

Keeping a journal is a time-honored means of self-discovery. Poet Deena Metzger says, "To write is, above all, to construct a self . . . [in response to] the most fundamental human need to know oneself deeply and in relationship to the world." Among the most versatile of written forms, a journal is an ideal place for self-exploration. There we may set our own rules concerning what we write, when, for how long, and why. Developing the habit of journaling gives us solace when we need it. It offers a safe place in which to try out new forms of self-expression, experiment with unfamiliar roles, or bring deeply held dreams and assumptions to light. Journaling teaches us to appreciate our unique life stories, even as it helps us become acquainted with previously unacknowledged habits of thinking, feeling, or acting.

Like other awareness practices discussed in this book, journal writing has a long history. For centuries people have kept journals, some of them simple logs of the day's events and others elaborate accounts that reveal much about the writer's inner life. Whatever the form, keeping a journal offers a way to respond to whatever touches us. Even if we do not think of our writings as "expressive"—in the sense of a literary creation, for example—when we write we have the power to give shape to something previously unsaid and perhaps unknown. When we write we draw upon a heritage so commonplace that we often take it for granted—our shared gift of language.

For even though we may not think of ourselves as writers, nearly all human beings are endowed with language. We begin even in the womb, as we learn the patterns and cadences of our mother's speech. We are welcomed into the human family with the words spoken around us at birth. Our early months are spent hearing and learning to imitate the sounds that will permit us to communicate with others in our world. As we get older, many of us become self-conscious about our abilities to use language well because schools place such a premium on speaking and writing according to specific rules and forms. Often we find the prospect of writing a story or poem or speaking in front of a group daunting, not to say terrifying. Yet even if our confidence has been eroded, keeping a journal offers one way to begin the process of

Journaling teaches us to appreciate our unique life stories

restoring our sense of wholeness by reclaiming this birthright.

How is journaling most effective in helping us to tend the seeds of our awakening? Like other practices that foster inner growth, journaling serves us best when it becomes a regular habit, which we are able to keep even when we do not feel like writing. At such times it is helpful to have a "bag of tricks," a set of exercises at hand that help us get started. A wide variety of written and taped resources can be found at most large bookstores, while many of the Integrative Practices found in this book may also stimulate the flow of ideas. Taking advantage of some of these apparently simple suggestions can bring new insights to the most experienced writers as well.

Even if we feel confident in our ability to get started, we may quickly feel stalled if it appears that others have access to our writings. It does not matter whether we plan one day to share what we have written. It is crucial to have a place where new beginnings can take form before we expose them to the less than tender mercies of the wider world. Our journals must offer us a private place, away from the eyes of others. When we feel safe enough simply to "go with the flow," we can entrust an emerging, perhaps barely identifiable feeling to paper. Then, if we are patient we can allow what we have written simply to be for a while, like a tender green shoot that needs time to grow before it can be transplanted.

Yet even if we can put our journals in safekeeping, we may also have to learn a deeper, more inward type of trust. Especially if we are new to journaling, we need to be patient with our feelings of awkwardness. We may have to suspend our doubts and judgment when we attempt to speak frankly about ourselves on the blank page before us. Some common techniques used in journaling, such as creating inner dialogues or listmaking, can seem pointless unless approached with a willingness to experiment. If we are prone to feeling self-conscious while writing, we have to give the practice some time before it begins to feel natural. Developing a sense of trust in the process is like developing trust in another person: many "conversations" are needed before we feel truly at ease when sharing something in confidence.

At its best, keeping a journal is a way to discover the gifts of solitude. As inheritors of language, we spend our days bombarded by an endless stream of partly verbalized thoughts, feelings, fantasies, and plans. At the same time we often are ignorant about what is truly important to us and fearful of being left alone, wary of where our minds might take us if left unguarded. Along with the other contemplative practices described in this book, journaling gives us the opportunity to begin to know ourselves, not simply as a collection of likes, dislikes, and personal anecdotes but as beings endowed with the ability to attend to the richness of human life. When approached with mindfulness, journaling also offers opportunities to be aware of the present moment as we write. This type of attention brings us back to the core of our being, even as we follow the movements of thought, feeling, and memory by tracing them on paper.

Like life itself, a journal is a work in progress. Whatever the contents, a journal serves as a light-sensitive surface capable of reflecting our state of mind with incredible nuance. The end product, whether written text or a largely blank page with a few scrawls, evokes the process of creation itself. Looking at a brief description of a scene written years earlier, the journal keeper enters a world created by his or her words. At the same time re-reading old journal entries may take a person deep into the mood that accompanied the writing. It may awaken old emotions or stir a sense of curiosity about forgotten details. In this way, a journal can become a vivid record of the inner upheavals that accompany seemingly imperceptible shifts in awareness or behavior. Then our journals remind us that attention to the inner life can bear fruit in all dimensions of our being.

Journaling gives us the opportunity to begin to know ourselves . . . as beings endowed with the ability to attend to the richness of human life.

Consciously attempting to put these fleeting thoughts into words offers an important vehicle for awareness. When we struggle in this way to convey our feelings—not to another, but to ourselves, the only designated reader of this document—we learn to pay attention and focus inwardly, with the "listening heart," as it is known to the contemplative traditions. When we give form to the formless ideas and feelings that accompany us through life we may for the first time begin to see them more clearly. Only then are we able truly to honor them and give ourselves permission, if needed, to let them go.

∾

Integrative Practices

Timed Writes

Timed writes are typically short bursts of writing designed to get your thoughts moving. Any word or phrase that comes to mind is fair game, even a phrase from a song that has been running in your head. Give yourself a specified amount of time—five minutes is a good starting point. Actually set a timer, so that you do not have to keep looking at the clock. The rules of the timed write are simple. Begin writing and keep going, not stopping to look back or lifting your pen from the paper. For example, you might begin with the word "cloudy": you free associate with that word. If you find that you are stuck, you simply repeat the word until something else comes to mind. Timed writes teach you how to "take dictation" from what your mind is saying. Later, if you wish, you may go back and reread what has emerged from this seemingly insignificant starting point.

One lead into a timed write used in many situations, is to

begin writing about yourself with the phrase, "Once there was a woman/man who. . . ." Take five minutes and write, allowing your mind and heart to take you where they want to go.

Letters to Yourself

Your journal is a wonderful place to come to terms with the people in your life. Writing a letter that you do not intend to send to someone with whom you have unfinished business can be especially helpful in clarifying your feelings.

A variation on this idea is to write a letter to yourself as a child. From the vantage point of the present, tell that child about his or her life to come, sharing the wisdom you have gained while keeping in mind the wonderment you carried with you when you were very young.

Learning Trust

A PERSONAL ODYSSEY
PAULA W. JAMISON

Some people approach the notion of keeping a journal with fear, or at least a degree of self-consciousness. When I was eleven, I was given a small book bound in red that could be shut with a tiny golden lock. A delicate little key came attached to it with a fragile chain. The cover bore the words, "My Diary" stamped in gold. Each page held a date, a page for each day of the year. A full page to fill with writing about the day's events! I don't know whether it was the rigidity of this format that filled me with such apprehension, but I recall being flooded with questions as I leafed through this new book that both beckoned and terrified me (a feeling that was to become distressingly familiar as I grew older and had to spend increasing amounts of my time writing papers for school). Did I have to fill *every* page of this diary? What if nothing happened on a particular day? Could I leave that page blank?—and wouldn't that mean that I would end up with a lot of blank pages? Or what if I had a special day—one of those early autumn days when the sunshine turns the leaves into amber and each smell, each touch of the wind, each sound struck my heart and senses with such force that I wanted to sing and dance and shout and repeat to all who could hear the stories the trees were telling me—on a day like that wouldn't I need at least three pages to record the glories I witnessed?

The word "Diary" struck me with glorious solemnity. At the time I didn't know it, but I was responding to something that was bigger and older than I, and I was teetering on the brink of entering a writer's world. Where better to begin, than with a pen and this simple book, which had come to me unbidden? At the same time, I saw that this book, with its little lock and key that supposedly made it into a repository of secrets, was emblazoned with an embarrassingly public declaration of its purpose. The puny lock, I immediately ascertained, could be picked by anyone with a bobby pin, a fact my brothers would be quick to notice. And the boldness of the gold lettering on the cover, combined with the ineffectual attempt at secrecy, made me uneasy. What if I didn't have anything to say that merited all this fuss? What if I didn't have any secret boyfriends to write about, or anything really REALLY special to say? What if my heart was empty and my senses dull? What if I couldn't live up to the promise of this blank book?

Anne Frank, the young Jewish girl whose diary of her years in hiding in Nazi-occupied Amsterdam had received great public acclaim in the 1950s, didn't help me one bit with my ambivalence about keeping a journal. I had learned about her story at an early age and wanted to imitate her. I had received the first of several blank books at the age of eleven or twelve, just as I was coming to know of her story and was plotting to get my hands on her famous *Diary* and read it for myself. Despite my good intentions about writing, however, all those clearly marked, ready-made books languished largely unused and were a source of nagging, niggling guilt, like a thank-you note that didn't get written to a great aunt. Yet it was quite clear to me that if a thirteen-year-old girl like Anne Frank could write a diary, I ought to be able to do the same.

I liked her idea of writing to her imaginary friend, Kitty, but try as I might I couldn't create or sustain that kind of written relationship with any of my imaginary friends. In fact, in those days, I was never sure who or what I was supposed to be writing *for*, and it was a long time before I found a way to be comfortable in the presence of a notebook all my own (without preprinted dates, to be sure). It took years before I found a way to write to and for myself, years before I understood deeply, in my heart, how much pressure I was putting on myself by thinking that what I wrote had to be like anything written by anyone else—even a young girl my own age.

Now when I take pen in hand and turn to my journal, I seldom fret about who will read me or where all these hastily written or painstakingly crafted pages will end up. When I feel the need to write, usually it is because I know that it offers me a way *to be present* with thoughts or feelings that have eluded me at other times during the day. Although I admit that it took time to set aside my visions of an idealized writer who hampered my imagination by seeming to spy on my every choice of word, now I write alone—not to bring to life some fixed notion of who I am or ought to be but instead to offer my attention in the best way that I can to the simple ordinariness of being alive.

Reclaiming the Artist Within

GAYL WALKER

The urge to create art forms that can be seen and touched is as old as humanity itself. Early men and women drew on cave walls for reasons that remain obscure to us today: perhaps to invoke luck in the hunt or to communicate with the gods. For at least a thousand years Tibetan monks have used mandalas—elaborate circular drawings—as a focal point for meditation and to direct spiritual energy. Native American medicine men have made elaborate sand paintings to heal specific ailments. Masks were worn by African witch doctors in rituals to cure illness. All over the world, human beings have made art to invoke sacred power. The beauty of nature seems to inspire in us a connection with something larger and more powerful than ourselves.

Until the industrial age, all human creations were made by hand rather than machines. Lacking hand work, once so central to our lives, we still yearn to make our individual mark. This need to create is a deep longing of the soul. In a world of manufactured clothing and household goods, we strive to express ourselves. People adorn themselves with jewelry and carefully styled clothing, create hairdos, and make up their faces. Some decorate their bodies with tattoos. The need to put our unique stamp on the world extends to our apartments, homes, and offices. We paint stripes on our cars and plant flowers around our houses and businesses. When we buy appliances or furniture, we are influenced by shape, color, and design. Some people will not buy a car that has everything they want if they do not like the color.

Seeing as an artist sees is something we all can do.

Many of us enjoy going to a museum or an art exhibit in a gallery. However, we usually participate as members of the audience rather than as the artist. Instead of decorating the house with our own art, we buy "real art" from a gallery. Once we got out of elementary school, we stopped putting our own art on the refrigerator, for by that time most of us had been sufficiently critiqued to shut the door to the joy of making art.

The realization that many of us think we are not artistic is disturbing. Thomas Moore writes in *Care of the Soul:*

> When we leave art only to the accomplished painter and the museum, instead of fostering our own artful sensibilities through them, then our lives lose opportunities for soul. To recover our artist self, we need to cultivate the artist within by giving it attention and living more artfully.

Reclaiming our artist-self can begin right here, right now. It begins with a shift in how we see ourselves. Try saying to yourself, *I am an artist.* It may feel odd at first, and it may take some practice to recognize its truth. But to begin, only your attitude stands in your way.

Seeing as an artist sees is something we all can do. To

encourage the artist that lies dormant within, it is only necessary to shift your vision. Then it is possible to practice seeing with an artist's eye. You can then nourish your artist-self by *paying attention* to the details of life around you. An artist's eye will see the many colors in a white flower, the way the light hits water, the curve of a child's neck, the sun illuminating fall leaves, the patterns in a rock. The artist's eye seeks out beauty and notices details and designs in nature.

This way of seeing is innate in everyone, but often lies dormant. When we were young we looked at and explored the world with excitement and wonder. As adults we still have this capability—we just need to remember, acknowledge, support, and take the time to see this way again. And we can only do this if we consciously slow down and look with awe. Racing through life fast-food style causes us to take our surroundings for granted.

When we see with an artist's eye, we recapture that childlike feeling of openness to our surroundings and appreciate the many marvels of creation.

Using ALL of your senses will help support and heighten this artistic awareness. Developing the capacity to be fully engaged in life is the key to living as an artist. You can practice by seeing all the colors in a sunset, listening to the sounds of birds outside, smelling the freshness of the air after the rain, touching the velvet of moss on a rock, tasting the sweetness of a ripe peach, or deeply feeling and acknowledging the emotions evoked by hugging someone you love. These are the raw ingredients, the foundation of a work of art. They are all part of our everyday lives: the details and the subtle nuances that we will see only if we wake up and honor them. When we see with an artist's eye, we recapture that childlike feeling of openness to our surroundings and appreciate the many marvels of creation.

This spirit of wonderment enriches our experience of viewing the art found in galleries or books. Approached with imagination, the works of others are no longer passive entertainment but allow a privileged glimpse through the eyes of the artist. As you position yourself in front of a painting, you are standing in the

place of the artist and are invited into his or her personal world. I have a prolific moonflower plant in my garden. Each time I go out to check for opening buds, I see the plant through Georgia O'Keefe's eyes, because she once painted a huge single moonflower blossom. How many people over the centuries have looked upon the Mona Lisa and made up stories about her life and mood? Looking at art enlarges our view. It is a way of knowing that does not use words. It goes beyond or beneath language to evoke feelings and tell stories. Art enters our being on a profound level and helps us better understand life.

Art also captures the relationship between the artist's inner thoughts and his outer manifestation. To do this, the visual arts, for instance, are based on a visible language with a vocabulary of color, line, space, texture, shape, and symbol. When you draw or paint a picture, even using stick figures, you are communicating with yourself and others through this language. In this sense, it could be said that every work of art is a self-portrait.

In general, there are two ways to approach the making of art. The intention of the exhibiting artist is to explore technique and make a *product*. Using art therapeutically, however, does not necessarily require technique, talent, or training. Here the focus is on the *process* of personal communication with the inner self. The goal is self-discovery. As we bring our attention to the process of making art, we are invited to watch as our hands bring forth objects that tell us much about who we are. In this relationship between inner life and outward form, we may find the seeds of awakening.

Although we all have the power to see and express what we see, many people are thwarted by our culture's elitist attitude about art. The prevailing mythology has it that an artist is someone extraordinary who has the talent, skill, and ability to magically pour out art. We think that to be a painter or sculptor, for example, an individual must have polished his or her raw talent with years of training and knowledge of the many rules of composition, placement, color, and technique. This may be true for artists who exhibit. However, those of us who recognize that the process of making art can be a meditative experience and may offer a way to healing or self-exploration are free to focus on the delight of the act itself. Approached this way, the process of art making may become a spiritual experience that connects us with the Divine.

One woman—not a professional artist—but one who has discovered that the act of painting had the power to heal her, wrote about the importance of creative expression in these words:

> The most overwhelming experience of grief occurred when my grandmother passed away. It is a day that will forever be etched in my memory. I was with my grandmother until she took her last breath, as she had been there for me for my first breath nineteen years earlier. She was my support, my best friend, and my own personal savior. When it came to a crashing end that December morning, I looked for comfort and found it in painting.
>
> I needed a form of expression more then ever now, to get through this. I have always painted— if I can see something, I can put it on canvas. I had never before tried abstract or symbolic art until my grandmother's death.
>
> I found myself sitting in front of a large blank canvas with a full palette of paints at my fingertips. Something happened to me. I put away my watercolors that I had intended to use for the portrait of my grandmother and cracked open my acrylics which I had not used in a long time. Then I began to paint like I had never done before—an almost insane, psychotic frenzy. Bright, sharp images appeared before my eyes and it felt wonderful. I felt like a true artist for the first time in my life. The thought of my grandmother being in heaven captivated my every thought and it was transposed onto the canvas. I worked intensely for three days, and had it completed in time for the memorial. I consider it my best work. It helped me so much to do this.

It is a great relief to people when they are given permission to let go of their expectations and just play with art materials. Being able to let go and surrender to the wonder and joy of the process allows us to find freedom of expression and can turn down the volume on the inner critic, that part of ourselves that likes to judge and analyze the product.

We can find joy in making art if we approach it from a child's point of view. Watch children draw with crayons and you will understand. Their art tells stories about their lives and the world of fantasy. Often they are content just to make marks, squiggles, dots, and lines as they explore and interact with the materials. They often seem to be asking, "What will happen if I do this?" They are in control of the crayons and can create any kind of world they want. There is magic and pleasure in this way of being creative. Once we learn to trust the process we can find comfort, satisfaction, and insight.

We now know that art can play an important role in healing, both emotional and physical. We have the innate need to express ourselves, to discover who we are, to bring meaning to the situations in our lives, and to tell our stories. We want to respond to life and reflect on it. But there are times when words are not adequate and we cannot express that which is most deeply held inside. Turning to a brush, marker, or clay may allow us to explore these feelings honestly and directly. Using creative expression as an outlet can be a valuable way to explore the inner self and understand feelings.

Making art leads to self-understanding. Approaching issues, problems, or emotions through the door of art may help us go deeper than we might if we were using words. Art work is a direct bridge to the unconscious and often shakes loose thoughts that are unspoken or unexpressed. In other words, art makes the invisible visible.

Art also has the power to help us "move through" emotions that we have been unable to acknowledge or release in other ways.

Art work is a direct bridge to the unconscious and shakes loose thoughts that are unspoken or unexpressed

Many times we have been taught to fear and avoid our feelings, especially our anger. However, there is nothing wrong with being angry. The difficulty arises when we get stuck, and instead of finding a channel for it we dismiss it or pretend that it does not have any power over us. Painting anger in bold, splashy red brush strokes often helps us act out and move through intense feeling. Expressing strong emotions in art (color, line, and symbol) taps into primitive areas of the brain and helps release feelings that we may be too inhibited or socialized to express verbally. Pouring out these intense feelings on paper or in clay helps us discharge their energy.

At one time I ran a support group for children who had life-threatening illnesses. One of the things they liked to do was to create images of things that made them mad or afraid. They would draw quickly and boldly on "yucky" brown or gray paper. After these drawings were finished, they took great pleasure in ripping them up and burning the pieces in a fireplace. This activity became a ritual to express their fears and let them go. It helped them purge these feelings rather than letting them fester inside.

Sharing images and stories in a supportive group or with a friend can be an important part of the healing process. When we share, we realize that we are not alone. When sharing your work, you do not have to know *why* you drew a certain way. Often in later conversation some insights will surface—or someone else may point out something that you had not noticed. Sharing can be a difficult step to take, especially if you do not have confidence in your artistic ability.

I am an artist and I clearly remember the first exhibit of my work at a spiritual conference. I felt as if I was naked in a room of fully clothed people. All my vulnerabilities surfaced. I felt exposed. The next time was easier, and I gradually found my confidence.

Paradoxically, once we find the courage to be vulnerable, we discover a new freedom. We radiate our authentic selves.

Feelings can be explored using a variety of media. If you are intimidated about your drawing ability, try working with collage — it can be very satisfying, and result in a deep and meaningful experience. The process of finding images often results in surprises if you allow your intuition and spontaneity to guide your selection.

When I was diagnosed with breast cancer and was scheduled for a mastectomy, I made a breast collage as part of my healing process. This activity seemed very important because I wanted to explore the meaning of breasts. Gathering images from old *Playboy* magazines, women's magazines, bra ads, and photos of Barbie dolls, I realized the importance of this singularly female icon throughout the media, our culture, and to myself. The center piece was a photo of my daughter nursing just after she was born. I added other photos that showed the strength of my body. I cut out drawings illustrating a self-breast exam, mammography, and a surgical drawing of a mastectomy. The cathartic process took several days and helped me examine the meaning of what I was about to experience. It helped me deal with the loss of my breast and its impact on my womanhood.

If we allow ourselves the freedom to enter into art as play, we can begin to find the way back to a sense of wholeness. Whether we are ill or are at another crossroads in our lives, the visions we bring to life with our eyes, minds, and hands reveal the longing for expression that makes us human. Wisdom bearers in many cultures have noted the deep yearning we feel to love and to experience a palpable connection with the divine. Reclaiming our inner artist is one way to satisfy this urge of the spirit to discover itself through form.

Integrative Practices

Often, words just are not enough, or they keep us from seeing the issues before us in new, more insightful ways. When we respond to a visual image, we are literally using a different part of our brain to process the stimulus. Perhaps that is one of the reasons why the experience of shape, color, line, or texture can evoke new levels of understanding ourselves and others.

Symbol of Healing

Spend some time envisioning what healing means to you. Is it physical or spiritual? Where in your life are you seeking healing? Using any media—paints, crayons, objects from nature, clay, etc.—create your personal symbol of healing. What are the feelings or thoughts that occurred to you during this process? Keep your symbol where you can look at it and reflect. Note how your connection with this symbol shifts over time.

Stress and Peace Collage

Close your eyes and imagine what stresses you. Create a collage from images and words found in magazines, newspapers, brochures, or calendars. Begin without any preconceived ideas and allow images to evoke your feelings spontaneously. Feel free to add any extra materials that strike your imagination—personal papers, tickets, bills, natural objects such as leaves or feathers, or bits of colored tissue, fabric, or string.

Now imagine what brings you peace and serenity and create another collage representing these things.

What images or insights come to you during this process?

Sound, Music, and Healing

GAYL WALKER

Sound is all around us—we only need to listen to our environment to start to understand how it affects us. Right now, stop and listen. What do you hear? Can you hear the low buzz of the refrigerator, or the hum of a computer, the heat, or air conditioning? Many of us have become so accustomed to these noises that we no longer hear them. Or we may prefer to put on music to mask the irregular comings and goings of noises that would otherwise distract us. We may choose something predictable, such as music or a ticking clock, over the more random and mechanical blurting of the machinery we live with. In some places the advent of technology has created an ongoing cacaphony. Faced with this expanding amount of stimulation, we struggle, sometimes successfully, to "block out" the noises that distract us. But this effort has a cost, increasing our need for balance and just plain relief from all the racket.

We all need quiet in our life, and it seems more and more difficult to get away from certain sounds. The ongoing roar of the big city, with horns blaring from cars, buses, and taxis, or the almost inescapable sound of highway traffic affects us all. At times nearly all of us can understand why "road rage" has become a topic in the news. Being in an unfamiliar environment also highlights our awareness of certain sounds.

Awhile ago, when I was recovering from surgery, I was very aware of the noises in the hospital: people talking, metal beds being moved down the hall, the clatter of meal carts and trays, the beeps of the IV pumps and heart monitors, even the squeak of rubber-soled shoes worn to muffle the sound of footsteps. The constant bustle was not conducive to my rest and healing. I craved peace and quiet and longed for the comforting, soft, familiar murmurs of my home environment.

One way to find relief from all this stressful stimulation is to rediscover the sounds of the natural world. Go outside for a few minutes and simply listen. Can you hear bird calls? Is a dog barking or a cow mooing in the background? As you walk outside do you hear the crunch of leaves, or the swishing of grass or tall weeds? Now listen to your body. Can you hear your breathing?

Now, focus on your internal rhythms—your heartbeat for instance. Your heart has been beating its rhythm all of your life. When you are stressed or excited or afraid, this rhythm speeds up considerably. At times of rest or during meditation your heart rhythm slows. Similarly, the rhythm of our breathing quickens and slows, depending on our physical and emotional state. These ever-present physical rhythms furnish the beat of our activities. To forget or distort these rhythms is to lose an important link to the pulsing of the universe around us as well as within us.

One way to find relief from all this stressful stimulation is to rediscover the sounds of the natural world.

"Sorrow that is held in is sorrow. But sorrow that is let out is song," wrote poet Mark Nepo. Because it is so linked with emotion of all kinds, listening to music can call up long-forgotten memories. Think of a favorite piece of music. Can you picture when you heard it and why it is so important to you? What feelings are released when you hear this music? Twenty years ago I had a role in the musical, *Jesus Christ Superstar.* Now every time I hear any of the music from that show, whether I am standing in the grocery store or driving, I can see myself on stage, and remember who was standing near me. I can feel the heat of the spotlights and even see the dust motes that were in the air. The music brings back that whole experience. For some of us, a particular piece of music may be associated with our first love. When we hear that piece, we are flooded with all the emotions associated with that relationship.

Music has profound effects on our nervous and hormonal systems, and has been used to enhance healing. Music can boost the immune system and regulate stress-related hormones. In one study at Michigan State University, research showed that listening to music for as little as 15 minutes a day can increase the levels of interleukin-1 in the blood. The immune system can also be strengthened by chanting, singing, or other kinds of vocalizing that increase oxygen to the cells. Blood pressure can be affected by sound and music. Exposure to excessive noise will elevate the blood pressure as much as ten points. People with high blood pressure who listen to lullabies and other slow relaxation music have been able to reduce their blood pressure.

Some surgeons now play music for their patients before and during surgery to alleviate anxiety. Music also has been found to reduce the need for pain medication and/or sedation. If you know you are going to undergo surgery, you may want to discuss with your doctor the possibility of playing your favorite kind of relaxing music in a tape player, using headphones during the procedure.

Even though you will be anesthetized, your body-mind will respond subliminally. A study in Texas showed that half of the women who listened to music during labor did not require anesthesia. Other researchers noted that music stimulation increases endorphin release which leads to a decreased need for medication. It also provides a distraction from pain and can relieve anxiety. In the same vein, studies of Alzheimer's patients show the power of music to stir up old memories. These patients, who are unable to speak, were exposed to favorite songs from earlier periods in their life. Listening to the familiar melodies, they were able to remember and sing all the words.

If you are sad and yet cannot turn on your tears for relief, listening to sad music may help you unleash your emotions. Conversely, if you are feeling down, uplifting music may make it easier for you to move out of your state. Listening to music in a dentist's chair helps to calm you. Your brain will automatically entrain, try to harmonize, or be in "synch" with the music, thus supporting your body to relax. This concept of entrainment allows us to understand why brain waves, respiration, heart rhythms, and even blood pressure can change when we listen to music.

The emotional power of music has ensured its role in many rituals and celebrations. A birthday party is not complete without singing "Happy Birthday." We feel patriotic when we hear the "Star Spangled Banner." Much of the great European music from the Middle Ages through the eighteenth century was developed to convey religious teachings or liturgy. Churches continue to use hymns as a form of worship, while weddings and funerals each have their own style of music. Music has great power as a cultural tie that brings us together and marks events in our lives.

This urge to punctuate life's occasions with music is found all over the globe. Indigenous cultures, which have lacked the high level of sensory stimulation provided by the mass media in the modern world, have given great emphasis to the power of song or drumming. Music could be used to usher in sacred moments or connect human beings with the world of the spirit. The way music can be used as a means to an almost sacred connection is touchingly illustrated in a story told by Jack Kornfield in *A Path With Heart*:

> There is a tribe in east Africa in which the art of true intimacy is fostered even before birth. In this tribe, the birth date of a child is not counted from the day of its physical birth nor even the day of conception, as in other village cultures. For this tribe the birth date comes the first time the child is a thought in its mother's mind. Aware of her intention to conceive a child with a particular father, the mother then goes off to sit alone under a tree. There she sits and listens until she can hear the song of the child that she hopes to conceive. Once she has heard it, she returns to her village and teaches it to the father so that they can sing it together as they make love, inviting the child to join them. After the child is conceived, she sings it to the baby in her womb. Then she teaches it to the old women and midwives of the village, so that throughout the labor and at the miraculous moment of birth itself, the child is greeted with its song. After the birth all the villagers learn the song of their new member and sing it to the child when it falls or hurts itself. It is sung in times of triumph, or in rituals and initiations. This song becomes a part of the marriage ceremony when the child is grown, and at the end of life, his or her loved ones will gather around the deathbed and sing this song for the last time.

Though it evokes a faraway culture, this tale speaks to our own lives as well. Each being, we are told, is endowed with his or her own song. When we give "voice" to this song we are brought into contact with our essential nature. In coming to recognize and celebrate our unique music, we are able to be who we are. Our music it enables us to touch and be touched by the hearts of those around us. Being able to sing our song literally and figuratively brings us into harmony with ourselves and the world.

❧

Integrative Practices

Sound is so omnipresent in our lives that we may actually spend much of our time screening it out rather than truly listening.

Meditation with Music

At a time when you have no distractions, listen to a piece of music that you enjoy or find meaningful. Give it your full attention—you may close your eyes if you wish. If after a time you notice you have stopped paying attention to the music and are lost in thought, simply go back to the sound.

Where did the music carry you?

Life Rhythms

What is the rhythm of your life? Is it fast or slow, or variable? What ways could you use to express this rhythm in order to give yourself more clarity?

Do you want to change the rhythm? What would it be?

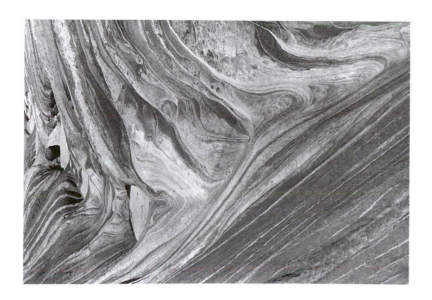

Rhythms of Life

A PERSONAL ODYSSEY
Gayl Walker

I became aware of the fast pace of my life after I was diagnosed with cancer. I contemplated the meaning of this illness and wondered what message it had for me. The connection between my life's rhythm and what my body needed to heal became apparent to me, and I understood in a new way how one rhythm influences the other.

Through poetry I began to explore what it felt like to experience the current rhythm of my life and to imagine a new, more healing rhythm.

The Rhythm of Disease *(staccato)*
    Frenetic, frantic
    Out of control.
    Runaway rhythm
    Cramming it all in
    Out of breath
    No time for breathing
    Not enough time to do
    Everything there is to do
    Never missing a beat
    Squeezing time
    Filling in the gaps
    Doing three things at once
    Running on empty
    Tight as a drum
    Sharp peaks
    I can do it all.
    Living on adrenaline.

I began to imagine what a new, more healing rhythm to my life would be:

"Healing Rhythm" *(legato)*
    Slow
    Soothing
    Flowing
    Refreshing
    Melodic
    Harmonious
    Nurturing
    Savoring
    Relaxed
    Being
    Living in peace.

This cancer was telling me something. I needed to pay close attention to the message I was hearing. It would have been easier to stay with the old rhythm, but there was an urgency to change.

Finding a New Rhythm

> The message is loud and clear
> Slow down the pace
> Make more whole notes
> Add rests and silence to the score.
> I'm stuck in the groove of a rhythm too fast
> Not wanting to miss a beat.
> A whirling dervish
> So caught up in the fast dance
> That the world is a blur.
> A habit developed and fueled by culture
> Status measured by accomplishments.
> Healing requires new music
> Illness has spoken its directive
> And I have chosen to listen.
> To find the song of the stillness.
> To see the beauty of a flower growing
> To hear the wings of the butterfly
> To relax in the symphony of life.

Through my own process and in teaching others, I have discovered that paying attention to our inner, spontaneous rhythms opens us to the potential for healing. Likewise, we can use this awareness to "atune" ourselves to others and, at the same time, discover ways in which sound and music can bringing healing into our lives.

Awakening through Movement

BARBARA TOSHALIS

Movement communicates life. Our breathing, the expansion and contraction of the body as it takes in and releases air, and the flowing of nourishing, cleansing blood confirm that we live. These basic movements accompany us throughout all of our days and unite us in the wonder of life. To be fully alive, however, we move not only to function, to get from one place to another, and accomplish tasks. We also move in response to joy, sorrow, celebration, and inspiration. To move and "to be moved" awakens the body, mind, and spirit to fulfillment. "To be alive is to breathe. . . . To breathe is to move, to move is to change. . . . "

For centuries, people have celebrated transitions with dance or movement. As the seasons changed, working our bodies rhythmically, we planted or brought in the harvest. We marked marriages, even death, with processions and dancing. To heal ourselves and those we loved, we made pilgrimages on foot to holy sites. We offered prayers with the movement of our breath or by our posture, reaching for support and answers, knowing we were integrally related to each other and to the Cosmos.

Modern life tends to repress these inherent needs to move. In response to stress, fear, and social pressures, we restrict our breathing and control how we carry ourselves. How often do we tell our children to be still, or to sit or stand in ways that our culture considers appropriate? Felt over a lifetime, these constraints can have a physical outcome, determining how we access our world. They have an emotional impact, for our capacity to move is closely linked to our sense of freedom and independence. Blocking our natural inclination to move reduces our capacity to give full expression to who we are and how we feel.

Physical and emotional trauma can also lead us to adopt a defensive posture, which may then be translated into our operative approach to the world and to the imagination. The process of aging, too, brings with it the loss of strength and flexibility, which can be further compounded by fears of injury or the adoption of self-imposed limitations. "Fifty-year-olds shouldn't dance like that," one woman mutters while watching a neighbor join her children on the dance floor. Yet beneath the fear that provoked her remark sounds a note of envy, perhaps even yearning.

In recent years, attention to ancient and newly emerging forms of movement has made it possible for us to find reunion with our deeper selves, where wisdom, healing, and creativity await our discovery. These forms may be explored by individuals alone or in groups. In either case, movement and dance methods facilitate our longing to connect with others. Whether we choose to experiment with spontaneous, expressive dances or adopt one of the ancient movement practices such as t'ai chi or yoga

To move and "to be moved" awakens the body, mind, and spirit to fulfillment.

posture flows, movement enables us to tap into awareness of the intimate yet often subterranean knowledge that we carry in our bodies. As we give ourselves permission to move, new energies for living and creating, for solving problems and dealing with conflict, come to the fore. For many of us, who have adopted sedentary adult lifestyles or confined ourselves to a few chosen forms of physical activity, allowing our bodies to move in new and perhaps unexpected ways makes it possible to rediscover the childlike pleasure of play.

When we free up our movements, new visions of what is possible for us and for the world are set in motion as well. Reaching into the wellspring of our creativity offers a means for healing our despair. If we regain the ability to jump for joy and collapse into sorrow, we become more fully alive, more authentic, and more playful. Living intentionally within our bodies, rather than in spite of our physical selves, we commune more fully with the natural world. We learn to honor our limits, and thus better understand the limits of others. In so doing we are able to participate more fully and creatively in our communities.

To regain our aliveness and the ability to be inspired by expressing ourselves through movement, we need a safe place with a welcoming atmosphere. For as much as we may long to break free of the constraints that hamper us, we also need to acknowledge our fear of spontaneity. Any loss of control can feel threatening, particularly at first. Privacy is crucial if practicing alone. If we choose to have music, it should reflect the desired mood. Only when such conditions are met is it possible to let one's fear soften. Then it becomes possible to gain the courage to move spontaneously.

Like other expressive arts, movement and dance can be vehicles for awareness. Psychotherapy has long recognized the specific importance of movement therapies, and with it the need to provide a supportive "space" in which the individual may feel at ease and open to new insight. Bypassing our habitual verbal responses, movement may lead us to the murky, often submerged memories and emotions lodged in the living tissue of the body. As one therapist notes,

> To nourish the core is to bring the body to consciousness, to invite the unconscious into embodied awareness. To do so calls for the need to make a space where one can listen to the body, a space for the body to speak *for itself*.

If we regain the ability to jump for joy and collapse into sorrow, we become more fully alive, more authentic, and more playful.

When we experience our bodies mindfully, as in the slow movements made during a yoga posture flow, or simply let ourselves follow the body's language as we respond to compelling music, we give ourselves access to a way of knowing that may otherwise remain beyond our reach.

The process of moving in order to awaken to the deeper self is an adventure. Each of us will make our own discoveries. Approaching such new activity wholeheartedly may lead to unforeseen results, as one woman discovered.

Anna had decided to participate in a workshop featuring expressive movement. For years she had struggled with her body image and an ingrained sense of herself as fat and clumsy. She was also an accomplished pianist. One day, "out of the blue," she told the group, she was inspired to try simple stretches and gentle rocking movements to a favorite recording of Debussy piano music. These were pieces that she had played many times and felt that she both loved and understood.

The experience was a revelation. "This music is slow and reflective," she told the others, "so I felt I wouldn't actually have to do much. But at one point I found myself standing and swaying like seaweed in the ocean. A whole world of memories flooded over me. I remembered being rocked as a small child by my old German grandmother. With that memory came such a deep sense of protection and belonging. I'd never felt anything like it before.

Then I remembered how much I loved that grandmother and the loss I felt when she died—I was eight at the time. I found myself brimming with joy, sadness, and gratitude all at once. I had no idea that those feelings were there."

Giving ourselves over to the experience of movement sounds as if it should be easy, and it may be for some. For others, even starting to move with awareness may be difficult. Beginning with simple, small movements—for example, trying the gentle swaying motions that Anna adopted or making tiny movements with our hands—offers a suitable starting point for those unaccustomed to expressing themselves in motion. For all of us, however, the first steps on the journey toward awakening through movement require a nonjudgmental attitude and a willingness to pay attention. In addition, any experience of movement is enhanced when we develop an awareness of the kinesthetic sense. This is how we experience movement and position, as well as the sensation of breathing. It is also helpful to try to come to a place of stillness, a deep relaxation of the mind and body, so that we can give our attention to impulses and images as they arise.

The first steps on the journey toward awakening through movement require a nonjudgmental attitude and a willingness to pay attention

When we give ourselves permission to move, we literally "set in motion" possibilities for developing our creativity and for healing. We can choose to dance alone to our favorite music or participate in a class. Each setting has its advantages. Moving within a group magnifies the energy available for each individual, especially if the leader is sensitive to individual needs and passionate about the work and play of creative movement. Moving in solitude may provide a sense of shelter and the spaciousness needed to explore new possibilities. If one is drawn to traditional forms of movement, such as t'ai chi, practice at home complements the time spent in class.

Whatever the context, when we approach movement with mindfulness and a sense of curiosity, we experience our body in new ways. Doors open to new understanding and images. We can then turn to other forms of expression—writing or the visual arts, for example—to bring our new discoveries into more lasting form. Then, returning once again to the experience of being in our bodies, we take what has come to us from our writing or drawing and expand it through movement. This interplay of forms evokes a spiral of growth, in which we bring to life newly emerging feelings, thereby deepening and clarifying otherwise fleeting intuitions.

When we give ourselves permission to move, we literally "set in motion" possibilities for developing our creativity and for healing.

As we experience our creativity, we use our bodies, hearts, and minds to bring something of ourselves into the world. We take the risk of moving and fully allow ourselves to attend to and respond to what our bodies convey. Responding to our sensing selves with all of our faculties, we listen and respond, listen and respond. We engage with the flow of previously unseen or unheard feelings and perceptions. We respond to the situations and objects we create and set loose in the world. And we dance—sometimes literally but always figuratively—with the people who surround us. Our movement through life is literally *embodied* in these and other forms of relationship. And as we move in relationship we are able to bring our creativity into ever widening contact with the world, to heal others and, most importantly, to heal ourselves.

Integrative Practices

We can experience mindful movement alone or with others. The practices described here, may be adapted to fit your needs.

Expansion and Contraction
Closing your eyes, focusing within, listening to your breathing, feeling the expansion and contraction of your body. Notice

what moves as you inhale. Then, as you exhale, notice how you take up less space, becoming smaller, shrinking. Allow your body to follow this natural rhythm, taking up as much space as you wish while you breathe *in* the air and energy from around you. Then take up as little space as you can when you *release* the old, stale air and thoughts. Keep your attention upon your movements, and sensations, as you feel your need to move or to be still.

Continue to allow your body to move in response to your breathing, exploring the floor, the room. Open your eyes only to move safely. Rest in stillness when your body directs you to do so. Notice how you feel. Note any images that come to you.

Attunement to the Natural World

This practice is most easily done out of doors, though with your imagination it can be carried out anywhere. Begin by taking a few moments to quiet the mind. If you are out of doors, simply allow yourself to open and receive the sights, sounds, and energies surrounding you. If inside, take a few moments to focus your mind on a natural setting that has moved you in the past. Allow yourself to experience this setting as fully as possible. In either case, notice what aspect of the natural world comes to your awareness. It could be a sensory impression, a memory, or an image. Consider the *qualities* of this aspect.

While standing, sitting, or lying down, begin to allow yourself to move in response to these qualities. Do not mimic or try to become this aspect of nature. Instead, allow your body to move *in honor of* the qualities this object has presented to you. Notice what comes into your awareness.

CHAPTER 5

Growing Together

Relationship and Healing

THOMAS HOLMES

How we live in relationship to ourselves and the world around us is a key component of health and healing. This is clearly articulated by Martin Buber. In his book, *I and Thou,* Buber suggests that the nature of our relationship with others and the world defines who we are. If we relate to others as whole persons, accepting and respecting all of who they are—in other words, if we see them as "Thou"—then in that act we ourselves are whole. If on the other hand we judge and analyze others, seeing them as things to be defined and studied as "Its," we ourselves become fragmented and compartmentalized. If we are whole and integrated, we will see the wholeness in others. This principle applies not only to our relationship with people but also to our relationship with the earth, to our sense of the divine, and with ourselves.

Our existence is shaped by the relationships that we have with all aspects of our lives. It is recreated at each moment that we relate to any part of our existence. In relationship to ourselves this means acknowledging as our own all those facets of who we are—the qualities that make us rejoice as well as those which we would sometimes like to forget. In relationship with others this means being able to relate to them in their entirety—not only the parts of the other person that are light and joyous but those that are darker or at times difficult for us to accept.

Relationship is about how we encounter the world, both inner and outer.

Relationship is about how we encounter the world, both inner and outer: how we respond to our sickness and aging or savor our health, how we grapple with our struggles or celebrate our successes. More conventionally, relationship is about how we bring our attention and caring to other people and to our physical surroundings. Each moment of contact is an opportunity to bring the practice of compassionate and nonjudgmental witnessing into our lives. Although it is sometimes difficult to recognize, we are constantly being invited to participate in life with our whole being. When we do so, we are *Thou* and the other is *Thou*—and for that moment we are whole.

This is no doubt what Carl Rogers was describing when he said that the most important thing in the counseling interview is not what the therapist says. Instead, what matters most is how congruent and present the therapist is and how he or she experiences the other person. Being nonjudgmental, as well as having "unconditional positive regard" and nonpossessive warmth, are essential to a therapist's effectiveness in facilitating the other person's integration and wholeness. If therapists only diagnose and use formulaic techniques, they are unable to bring about the kind of healing that research has shown occurs when counselors focus on being as fully present as possible. Indeed, many studies have demonstrated that the most important factor associated with positive change in psychotherapy is the quality of relationship. The type of therapeutic technique used has little effect on outcomes.

The formal relationship developed between counselor and client is only one way in which our innate capacities for relatedness bring change in our lives. The following sections explore the role of relationship and health. We open with a look at our innermost relationships, as we experience our emotions and our bodies. Then we broaden the perspective to examine a few of the myriad ways in which we relate to other people and to our environment. How we perceive ourselves in the world—whether we feel we belong to it or are isolated from it—plays a crucial role in our capacity to give and receive emotional and spiritual sustenance.

Connecting with Our Inner Selves

Thomas Holmes

In order to awaken to the possibilities of life, it is helpful to understand and explore the ways in which our inner selves are constructed. Although we often think of ourselves as having one personality, actually there are many components that make up the completeness of who we are. Our relationship to this complex array of inner selves sets the tone for all of the relationships in our lives. It serves as the foundation for how we relate to others. Unfortunately, many of us experience life situations that cause some parts of us to dominate our personality, at times leading us to lose touch with the essence of our being. When this occurs, the process of awakening requires that we reconnect with the parts of ourselves with which we have lost touch, allowing them to return to the surface of our awareness.

The initial step in this reconnection is to develop a relationship with our inner "selves" by understanding how these parts of ourselves operate in our daily life. As we move through the day we experience a variety of states of mind. We might call these good moods or bad. We may find ourselves "all business" one day and another day feeling "goofy" or "playful" and unable to get down to work. At other times our romantic side may emerge, or if we are rebuffed by someone we care about, a hurt child part of us may come forth. The human psyche is remarkable, for it is designed to allow these various states of mind to help us cope with the many facets of life.

These various mental states are referred to in different ways. Some psychologists call them subpersonalities, or more specifically, "parts" of our inner "family system" (Schwartz). They are also known as "archetypal patterns" (Jung), "our many faces" (Satir), and "schemas" (Piaget). Regardless of the term we choose, it is helpful to have a language to serve us in relating to the constant dance that occurs among these different aspects of our personality. We may find them rising up and falling back, coming into conflict with each other, teaming up with other parts, or sometimes being cast away into the depths of our psyche where they are rarely visited.

Especially since we are usually hesitant to embrace certain parts of ourselves, it is helpful to realize that all of these subpersonalities have positive functions in our inner system. The angry parts are there to protect us and set boundaries, the affectionate parts to establish intimate relationships, the judgmental parts to make good decisions, and the playful parts to help us relax and feel restored. While the original function of these parts is positive, however, they can also become extreme or rigid, which leads to an imbalance. We all know people who are locked into extreme critical parts, with instant judgments to offer on any subject, or people who are always in their serious working part and are unable to relax and play. In contrast, a healthy system of inner parts allows us to move from one part to another as needed.

Some people relate to the metaphor that likens their internal system of parts to software programs designed to help them cope with life's various tasks. In other words, we have a variety of icons that we may click on as needed—possibly a money manager part that comes in handy when it is time to pay bills, or a playful part that functions like a game program. While these various parts may be activated by particular activities or people (who "push our buttons," as it were), sometimes it is difficult to access the part of ourselves that we most need. We may need to activate our money manager but cannot seem to get out of the game program. Part of what we must learn in such situations is how to return to the "main menu," where we can see the icons of all the parts and access them.

When we are in the self we are able to observe the parts but are not taken over by them.

Another way of looking at the psyche is to see it as a garden and to be aware of the parts of ourselves that we are cultivating. What parts make up the garden? Is there a balance among them? Do important parts lack the space to grow? Are there parts that have become like weeds growing all over the garden, drawing nutrients from other plants? Such questions are a useful starting point for exploring our inner relationships and determining what steps need to be taken in order to cultivate the unique qualities that they bring to life.

Another effective way that we can become better acquainted with our most prominent parts is to select several situations that occur every day and carefully observe our habitual responses. When we do this, we see our parts in action. Similarly, reflecting on significant past experiences can provide us with important insight. These include situations in which people or circumstances activate certain parts, or solitary times in which it is possible to observe shifting moods coming to the surface. It is also helpful to list these observations, reflecting on the emotions, thoughts, and physical reactions that occurred at the time. Visual images may be more powerful than words at such times: drawing a picture of the part or finding a picture in a magazine may serve as an important reminder, especially when in the early stages of becoming acquainted with our various parts. Human and nonhuman forms or symbols may be used as well.

In the center of the inner system we experience something that is different in nature from the parts. This is the place from which we can observe our parts— it is the center of ourselves. In ego psychology it would be called the "observing ego." Buddhists refer to it as the "witness." Richard Schwartz, developer of the internal systems theory, refers to it as the "self." When we are in

the self we are able to observe the parts but are not taken over by them. For example, there are times when we may become so angry or sad that we are not simply angry or sad, we *are* anger or sadness. If we are able to step back from that state, perhaps because we practiced mindful breathing or because someone empathically reflected our sadness or anger, then we can get some distance from the engulfing emotion. In that moment the self comes to the foreground of our consciousness.

Another way to imagine the self is to see it as the conductor of an orchestra. The conductor blends together the sounds of all the different instruments to make music. There are times when the trumpets need to sound, and others when the violins play soft romantic music. The self has a similar role: to call forth the strong, assertive parts of us when we need to protect ourselves, or to soften our mood when we relate to loved ones.

Shifting from one state to another is not always easy. For

example, if we come home from work after being in our business manager part all day, we may not be able to respond with affection when our children come running up to us. Instead, we may ask them if they did their chores and give them directions about doing their homework before we even greet them properly. Some parents get so caught up in the role of nurturing their children that they have a difficult time disciplining them. The ideal is to have access to the widest range of states of mind so that we are not limited by having just a few sets of responses to life's varied situations.

As we develop the capacity to observe our parts, we find that we are more centered in our self. In this state, we are better able to stop automatic reactions that we may later regret. We are also better able to experience feelings of compassion, calm, and competence, along with a deeper understanding of other people.

How may we understand the elusive nature of this self we are describing? One of the best ways is through poetic imagery, with its capacity to evoke instead of simply naming. For example, in "Song of Myself," Walt Whitman vividly contrasts the qualities of that central self with his other "parts," which he begins by describing:

> My dinner, dress, associates, looks, business, compliments,
> dues,
> The real or fancied indifference of some man or woman
> I love,
> The sickness of one of my folks—or of myself . . . . or
> ill-doing . . . . or loss or lack of money . . . . or
> depressions or exaltations,
> They come to me days and nights and go from me again,
> But they are not the Me myself.
>
> Apart from the pulling and hauling stands what I am,
> Stands amused, complacent, compassionating, idle, unitary,
> Looks down, is erect, bends an arm on an impalpable
> certain rest,
> Looks with its sidecurved head curious what will come next,
> Both in and out of game, and watching and wondering
> at it.

The self is that place from which we can observe ourselves and the world in a nonjudgmental, curious and compassionate way.

Many other traditions around the world and throughout history have also attempted to communicate these qualities. For example, Steven Mitchell quotes Chuang-tzu, the Chinese Taoist master (369-286 BCE) describes the place of the observing self in the following passage:

> When we understand, we are at the center of the circle, and there we sit while Yes and No chase each other around the circumference.

In the great religious traditions, the individual self appears to be a doorway through which we may access the greater Self, which many call the experience of the divine.

The "parts" are those aspects of ourselves dancing around the ring, the yes and no chasing each other. We are in the self when we are in the center, or when we are Walt Whitman's "Me Myself." When Whitman depicts the self with the words, "apart from the pulling and hauling stands what I am, Stands amused, complacent, compassionating, idle, unitary," he is describing qualities that fit well with the characteristics of self mentioned earlier. In the self we are relaxed, assured, and able to listen and respond to feedback.

Psychosynthesis, a form of psychotherapy, offers an equally vivid albeit less poetic definition of self that highlights the same qualities. Here the self is defined by Brown as

> an integrating center which is the essential individual, underlying roles, behaviors, feelings, thoughts, physical manifestations, even gender. The self is a center of pure awareness and of intentionality, or will.

The self, then, is that place from which we can observe ourselves and the world in a nonjudgmental, curious, and compassionate way.

Many religious texts and poems express and expand upon this notion of self. In fact the states of mind valued by religious seekers of various traditions bear a strong resemblance to the qualities evoked to describe the individual inner self. Steven Mitchell cites the Mundka Upanishads where the self is described as not only the peaceful place in the center of our individual being but also as the locus of connection to the peace residing at the center of all things:

> Self is everywhere, shining forth from all beings, vaster than the vast, subtler than the most subtle, unreachable, yet nearer than breath than heartbeat. Eye cannot see it, ear cannot hear it nor tongue utter it; only in deep absorption can the mind, grown pure and silent, merge with the formless truth. As soon as you find it, you are free, you have found yourself; you have solved the great riddle; your heart forever is at peace. Whole, you enter the Whole, Your personal self returns to its radiant, intimate, deathless source.

Many meditative traditions encourage the cultivation of this place of stillness from which we witness ourselves and the world with nonjudgmental awareness. The Buddhist master Thich Nhat Hanh recommends attuning our consciousness with the practice of seeing the world with "compassionate eyes, looking at living beings." This description has much in common with states of mind sought after in many other religions. In the great religious traditions, the individual self appears to be a doorway through which we may access the greater Self, which many call the experience of the divine.

Integrative Practices

Exploring Your Inner System

In order to get to know our inner system, our inner "cast of characters," we can pay attention to the states of mind that arise as we go through the day.

What are the qualities of the states of mind or moods that

arise in different situations? What feelings or thoughts arise while you are in these different states of mind? How does your body feel when you are in a particular state of mind?

What seems to activate this part of yourself? When and how often do these parts appear? If you were to give this part of you a name, what would you call it? If you were to represent this part as a picture, what would it look like?

Recollecting the Self

Remember a time when you felt particularly whole and at ease in the world. It may have been a time you spent in nature or during a crisis, or a spiritual moment. What were those times like? What conditions supported those feelings? What words come to you that might go along with that experience?

Befriending Our Bodies

MOLLY VASS-LEHMAN

We usually go through the days and years of our lives not paying attention to how miraculously our bodies continue to function despite the stress and strain of daily living. It is easy to take our good health for granted, that we will feel well and have the energy to do the things we need and love to do. Injury or illness jolts us into the awareness of just how fragile our bodies can be. Even the simplest of tasks takes on mammoth proportions or becomes beyond our capacities. In the blink of an eye, our altered physical condition transforms the lens through which we view ourselves and the world around us.

Some people have spent much or all of their lives beset by physical or mental problems, while a fortunate few are able to enjoy vibrant health well into old age. But at some point all of us will be touched by illness, either our own or that of a loved one. How we come into relationship to our bodies, minds, and spirits in such times has a great impact on the quality of our lives. The experience of illness has the power to set loose our darkest fears, leaving us trembling at the discovery of our fragility and mortality.

It comes as no surprise that we may resist accepting the reality of a medical condition or react with anger and dismay when we are unable to obtain quick answers or relief from our suffering. Even with sophisticated medical technology, many diseases are difficult to diagnose. Relief from our suffering is neither simple nor immediate. We respond with frustration, longing for reassurance so that we may return to the flow of our accustomed routine.

The dark times of sickness have the power to leave us with wisdom and compassion.

When we fall sick, it is difficult to see what the experience has to teach us. We feel like an ant looking up at a huge neon sign, overwhelmed by its brightness and unable to understand the message. All we can do is struggle to keep up with the ever-shifting demands imposed on us by our changing bodies or the loss of our "normal" capabilities. Yet as time passes we may realize that we have come to understand something more about others and ourselves. The dark times of sickness have the power to leave us with wisdom and compassion. Whether we slowly lose our ability to function or are yanked out of our healthy everyday lives without warning, illness bears gifts to the unsuspecting. If we can move beyond our fears and self-preoccupation, our suffering can bring us a greater sense of empathy for others who contend with similar or more severe problems. It can also lead us to a sense of gratitude and renewed appreciation for each moment.

Whether we are aware of them or not, our reactions to illness are colored by deeply held beliefs. Illness brings to light our assumptions regarding what and whom we trust, as well as the very meaning of health. Our belief systems come to us in many ways: through our families of origin, the larger culture in which we live, education, and direct experience. To understand how we arrive at our private views of health we can look at our family histories, what we learned as children, and how we saw our parents approach their own health in times of wellness and illness. In addition to sharing genetic and lifestyle traits that might predispose them to certain illnesses or robust health, families transmit attitudes about how to behave when sick or even growing old.

Overall cultural attitudes also have a great impact on our perceptions of what it means to be healthy and how we should act when we are not. For most Americans, who are born into a culture that holds the paradigm of allopathic medicine as the model of health care, treatments based on this perspective offer the only effective remedies for the ailments that besiege them. Other cultures favor different views. Individuals raised in an environment that values homeopathy, which in many European countries coexists with allopathy, will have a different understanding of treatment options. Furthermore, they will make different assumptions about how the body works and responds to medicine. People who have grown up with ancient Asian conceptions of healing, such as Aryuveda or traditional Chinese medicine, will have an intuitive understanding of the body as an energy system that until recently seemed extremely foreign—and suspect—to most Westerners. Each system, then, is more than a collection of treatments or remedies. Instead, each reflects an underlying philosophy that envisions health and healing in a unique way.

Today, knowledge of these and other traditions has become available in the West. Many individuals and health care professionals who grew up with an allopathic background are integrating information and modalities from other perspectives into their views on healing. As a result, choices for treating illness or "optimizing" health have become increasingly complex.

Over the last decade, a new field, known as Complementary

Illness bears gifts to the unsuspecting.

Health Care, has emerged and quickly attracted the attention of mainstream society and the health care system based on the allopathic "medical model." The importance of this movement cannot be overestimated. From the growing interest in herbs to the widespread acceptance of massage, people seek to relate to their own health in a more multidimensional way.

Along with the expansion of choices come new challenges. Processing all that is available can be confusing and exhausting, especially in times of illness. If we are diagnosed with cancer, heart disease, or many other health problems, we are faced with so many treatment options that it becomes difficult to see what best fits our situation and underlying beliefs.

When we are ill, it is particularly important to remember to listen not just to those around us but to turn our attention inward. We must be reminded to give ourselves time to reflect as we move through the process of deciding what is best for our own health. We need to remember that we are each individuals with unique requirements, and that what works for one person may not help another. Ultimately, no one can tell us what choices will be best—and this is true both in times of illness or when we feel most healthy. A delicate balance is necessary to be able to detect our needs even as we absorb and evaluate the opinions of others. This is especially important when we are faced with our own "disease" and the fear or panic it may engender.

Being able to hold this balance is an important step toward freedom in our relationship to our own health. It is difficult to fathom the full miracle of the human body and the immense number and kind of functions it performs. For all that we know about human physiology, much is still a mystery. One thing is certain: like snowflakes, each body has its own unique pattern and make-up. At the cellular level, each body operates in an individual molecular balance with unique requirements that must be met if vital life functions are to be performed. Understanding the body

Our recognition of the body's wisdom cannot be static or rooted in concepts.

in this way opens us to a sense of awe and wonder—we are not exactly like any other person on earth. Each one of us is an important part of the whole mosaic of life.

Yet recognizing such subtle levels of difference also presents us with a challenge. How, then, are we to discover what this body needs to function at its best? In our society and its health care system, scientific evidence, based on large pools of data, is the basis for proposing general guidelines to all about nutrition, exercise, and other lifestyle factors. But with such great variations among individuals in the population, one person's needs may be vastly different than those of another. For example, Ellen may function best when she takes 500 mg of vitamin C a day, yet her husband may need as much as 5000 mg, depending on his state of health or illness. No set formula is right for everyone.

No doubt it would be easier simply to follow a prescribed program for our health, but matters are not that convenient. Unfortunately, in our consumer culture, based on the need for mass marketing, many books on diet and lifestyle appeal to this desire to keep things simple. Millions of copies are sold based on the tantalizing promise of clear-cut solutions to our health issues. Many people then try to follow diet or exercise plans that work for awhile but prove impossible to sustain over time. Many have also heeded stories about what helped in the healing of another person and tried the same approach, but to no avail. If we allow ourselves the time and space to listen carefully to the body and its wisdom, eventually it is possible to come to a deeper understanding of our unique requirements for health and healing.

Deep within us sounds an internal rhythm, a flow that moves our lives like a river of energy and sustenance that has its own timing and cycles. Perhaps it takes illness or growing older to begin to see the pattern of these inner processes in our lives and to accept our uniqueness. Then we learn to honor the body in all its strengths and weaknesses, its resiliency and fragility. This care-

At the cellular level, each body operates in an individual molecular balance with unique requirements that must be met if vital life functions are to be performed.

ful listening is another process of attunement, allowing us to hear the song of our bodies and to care for ourselves in ways that are appropriate to our needs of the moment. It takes the form of listening daily to the shifting rhythms of our life cycle. Responding to our bodies in this way is like a dance, in which we learn increasingly how to follow and trust the body's messages and to respond accordingly. It is then that we begin to experience a profound wisdom held in the body, a wisdom that is available to us when we are faced with choices about our health and healing.

Our recognition of the body's wisdom cannot be static or rooted in concepts. It demands instead that we engage in a process. For the body is always changing, every second that we are alive. Transformation is taking place at all levels, and part of us is constantly being born anew. Like a snake that sheds its skin in order to make room for new growth, we are constantly letting go of what no longer works for us. As we develop the capacity to experience our bodies on more subtle levels, we tap into this rich reservoir of information deep within. Each time that we come into a deeper understanding of what lies within us it brings us a kind of grace. With it comes a sense of humility, as we behold the miracle and mystery of the body and how it serves us. Humility also comes in the form of illness.

Paradoxically, pain and discomfort can help teach us a sense of reverence for our bodies or how to find a place of peace deep within. A comment made by a woman suffering from multiple sclerosis reflects the hardwon acceptance that illness can teach: "Each day I just put one foot in front of the other and try to find meaning and peace in that moment." Illness can profoundly change us and force us to slow down, to listen, and to follow. Although this woman did not set out to do so, she has found a deeper sense of her place in the universe through the process of coming into relationship with her illness. She has agreed, on some level, to heed the teachings she has received through her body.

❧

Integrative Practices

Listening reverently to the silent community within the body helps us attend to each member, both individual and in community with others.

Listening to the Wisdom of the Heart

The heart is an amazing organ that serves us day in and day out in miraculous ways. Yet it is also true that there are few organs in our bodies that respond so immediately to both stress and nurturing. Take time now to listen to the wisdom of your heart.

Relax. Find a comfortable rhythm for your breath. Attend. Draw your attention away from your breathing to your heart. Pay attention to what you notice about your heart and the area around it. What feelings or images come to mind? Then take a few moments to have a dialogue with your heart. What images or messages come from this dialogue?

Your Body

Take a few moments to reflect on your experience of the body. Where in your body do you feel the effects of stress? How do you care for yourself when you notice these signs of stress? Write a prescription for your self. What does your body need?

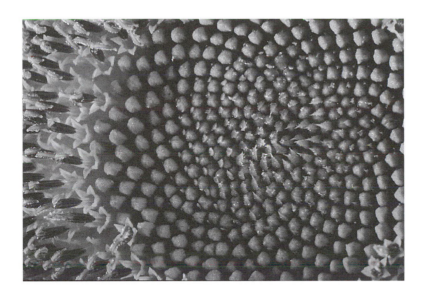

Journey through the Inner Labyrinth

A PERSONAL ODYSSEY

MOLLY VASS-LEHMAN

Like everyone else, I have had to learn things the hard way when I have not taken the time to pause to listen to what my body is telling me. This happens in simple everyday activities, such as when I push my body beyond its capacity in sports such as racquetball or running. Or I do not get enough rest because I try to fit too many things into a day. Then I end up suffering the consequences for days or even months afterward. At times I have also listened to others tell me what is best for my body or have even allowed them to harm my body in the name of helping. In fact, as I write I am steeped in the experience of an illness that began without warning.

It started innocently enough—a slight dizziness through the afternoon. By evening it had progressed into a terrifying experience that continued throughout the night. At first, I thought I was having a stroke. I felt the room spinning out of control and I found myself unable to stand or walk. My head was pounding and my eyes would not focus. I called to my husband to tell him what was happening and then tried to go to bed to see if the episode would subside.

Instinctively, out of fear I went into our meditation and prayer room to get a small icon of the Virgin Mary that my husband had brought me from a recent trip to Russia. I set it beside the bed and started reciting the "Hail Mary" over and over. This seemed odd to me, as I am not Catholic and do not say this prayer with any regularity. However, over the next five or six hours I said the prayer as the vertigo continued. In the terror of the night it seemed like the only thing I could do to feel a sense of safety.

Over the next few days I tried in desperation to find out what was wrong. From visiting the emergency room at the local hospital to calling my homeopathic physician, I searched in vain for the answer to my problem. Fortunately, I shared my story with the wife of a colleague and she told me about her recent experience with vertigo. She gave me an article she had found on the Internet about a condition affecting the inner ear known as Benign Paroxysmal Positional Vertigo, or BPPV. As soon as I read the first few paragraphs I realized that what I was experiencing could be traced back to a preventive dental procedure I had undergone shortly before the dizziness began.

At the dentist's that day I was in an inverted position with my head about two feet off the ground and my feet in the air. The dentist opened and closed my jaw with great force for nearly two hours. Midway through the process I expressed my concern to the dentist, asking him if this procedure could hurt me. "No," he said, "the skull is too strong." What I did not know at the time was that such force could damage the inner ear. The pressure caused the tiny calcium crystals within it, which convey to us our position in space, to shift position. This, I later discovered, was the root of my problem. It was one of those times when I did not listen closely enough to the inner cry of my body. Instead I let the opinion of a health care professional override this wisdom. It has been a painful lesson, but one that has brought me a greater understanding of myself than I could have ever imagined.

I find it interesting that this disorder is sometimes referred to as "labyrinthitis." While the term is intended to refer to the intricate semicircular canal system of the inner ear, it also offers a powerful metaphor for our inner journey. In this instance I have entered the labyrinth of illness and have come face to face with the gifts and challenges of living out my call on the earth.

Day by day I am learning to cope with a disorder that literally and figuratively upends my sense of balance. I am forced to stay grounded. Sometimes it feels as if I am in the middle of a story by the well-known author and neurologist, Oliver Sacks. While for much of the time I cannot appreciate the process I am undergoing or get a sense of its underlying meaning, I am slowly beginning to catch glimpses of what it brings up in my own psyche and spirit.

Vertigo also offers an important metaphor for my life. Vertigo occurs as the body attempts to find a place of equilibrium, or balance. In my case the brain is sending a message that the world around me is moving. This is the result of a process involving these small crystals, which have shifted out of place and affected my experience of balance. In response to this distorted perception, the eyes involuntarily begin to roll, while balance, eyesight, memory, and other vital functions are affected.

A chronic or acute disorder immediately prompts us to try to find a way to adjust to our new relationship to our environment. There is the wish to continue to participate in our daily lives, our work, our relationships, and the things we love to do. Our initial response to such an alteration in our normal flow of functioning is to try to find a way to bring ourselves back to a familiar and normal way of being. But in many instances this is physically impossible. Instead, as we begin to accept the alteration the body miraculously finds other ways to carry out the functions we need and want to perform. Observing our adjustment is like watching a masterful artist create a new picture of how we can act and respond. We begin to find unimagined inner resources for coming into relationship to this new challenge.

At times like this, we feel a sense of awe. Our trust in the body's capacities deepens. It is as if we are watching a beautiful dancer intuitively seeking the right footing in rocky, uncharted territory. In my experience of vertigo, for example, my brain has had to learn to process sensory information in a new way to compensate for the lost sense of balance. My eyes make multiple adjustments, while simultaneously my other senses become more acute in order to keep me functioning as well as I can. My conscious, thinking mind has no part in this incredible series of shifts and recalibrations. At such moments I feel that in truth I am being led by the body's wisdom. My role is to follow.

Surrendering to the flow of this dance requires trust, humility, and the acknowledgment of grace. We spend so much of our lives believing that we are the drivers of body, mind, and spirit. Yet at times like this we are catapulted into the awareness that we are just part of the dance. It is our responsibility to participate in the process, but we do not have to—and in fact cannot—do it all. We come to the realization that our will alone, no matter how strong or determined we are, cannot heal us. It is the intimate relationship between will and grace that will pull us through. True healing and freedom emerges from this place of response, in which action and surrender are both present.

This dance is an ongoing process. There will be times when

we feel encouraged and full of hope. There will also be times of frustration and despair. This ebb and flow is a natural part of all of our lives—in sickness and in health. How we come into relationship to this dance brings richness and deep meaning into our life's journey. Our relationship to our bodies and our deepest innermost selves colors our engagements with the people around us. It forms a subtle undercurrent to our outgoing, "public" selves as well as to our most intimate ties with loved ones.

Honoring Others

KAREN HORNEFFER-GINTER

Given that we live in a culture that focuses on the individual, it is not surprising that when concepts of awakening or spiritual practice are considered, they are often framed as solo activities. In many ways this makes sense. If we are to listen within, we need time alone to return to our inner stillness. If we are to find balance amidst the hectic pace and over-stimulation that fills our days, we require retreat and solitude. As essential as this yearning to be alone is, however, we often long to find deep connection with others as well. Our relationships with others and our involvement with the world often complement our inner seeking, framing our life with meaning and purpose.

Not only do our relationships provide us with a sense of

belonging and meaning but they also challenge us to extend ourselves to others. In so doing we stretch our capacities for acceptance, patience, and tolerance. Such sentiments have more recently been echoed by researchers across a variety of fields. The quality of our friendships, the satisfaction we feel in marriage, our sense of belonging to communities—these factors all contribute to our feelings of happiness and fulfillment in life. Moreover, existing evidence also suggests important connections between our social lives and our physical health. For example, the presence of social support increases one's odds of surviving breast cancer and decreases the incidence of heart disease among those who are at high risk. It has even been suggested that the power of love and intimacy has as important an impact on the incidence of disease as diet, smoking, exercise, stress, genetics, drugs, and surgery.

These findings are interesting in themselves. However, it is also noteworthy to consider the attention devoted to examining the power of relationship. What does it mean when we as a society require elaborate studies to remind us that relationships are powerful and healing? Have we moved so far into an individualistic sense of survival that the importance of receiving and giving love is now headline news?

Even without such scientific evidence, most of us have had life experiences that illuminate the power invested in relationship. There is nothing that stirs human emotion as much as our connections with others. Relationships provide us with our happiest memories in life: falling in love, being called a best friend, finding a group of people among whom we feel at home. They also require us to endure the challenges inherent in relating to others: to risk the possibility of experiencing the ending of love, the betrayal of a friend, or the grief of losing a loved one. It is from relationships that we receive many of the essential ingredients of our functioning: support, feelings of being understood,

The quality of our friendships, the satisfaction we feel in marriage, and our sense of belonging . . . contribute to our feelings of happiness and fulfillment.

and a sense of belonging. Relationships also provide us with opportunities to grow and learn from the challenges of life. Grief, loss, loneliness, or isolation often teach our hearts compassion.

Certainly relationships take on many forms, from dyads—such as friendships, intimate partnerships, and parenthood—to larger groups including extended family and community organizations. In a sense, each of these forms can be seen as an extension of our core relationship with self. It is often said that we must first be able to love ourselves in order to fully give or receive love from another. From this type of self-love and acceptance comes our ability to respect and honor others fully, and to discern the type of relationships we want to have. In turn, it is often our ability to embrace another, to accept this person totally, that allows us to embrace our own wholeness. For example, in the act of accepting another person's sadness or anger, we allow ourselves the freedom to feel the same emotions.

Our relationship with the self serves as a foundation for our relationship to others. Many times the culmination of our inner work is the discovery of how to express ourselves authentically in relationship. Our individual spiritual practices, such as meditation, movement, journaling, or other types of creative expression, may lead us to view our connections with others in a new light, as a rich opportunity for conscious attention. The fluid nature of genuine relationship repeatedly forces us to confront ourselves and one another. When it is undertaken consciously, relationship is a natural evolution of the process of awakening. And in this sense it has been termed one of the true tests of spiritual practice. The challenges inherent in choosing to be involved with others is also highlighted by Starhawk:

> It is easier to be celibate than fully alive sexually. It is easier to withdraw from the world than to live in it, easier to be a hermit than to raise a child, easier to repress emotions than to feel them and express them, easier to meditate in solitude than to communicate in a group.

When it is undertaken consciously, relationship is a natural evolution of the process of awakening.

One reason that bringing spiritual awareness into our relationships with others is such a challenge is that most of us spend so much time with other people. To choose consciously to be in relationship is to choose to be conscious *throughout* the day. We make the commitment to be fully present with our loved ones, acquaintances, and the people we encounter casually. How we relate is an outgrowth of the mindfulness practices described elsewhere in these pages. It could even be said that embracing relationship as a spiritual practice requires expanding our awareness and attention to cultivate a quality of *heartfulness*. This may take the form of greeting others with the expression "Namaste," meaning, "The light within me honors the light within you." It may also be expressed by praying for another's highest good, or by the simple act of listening attentively and respectfully. Whatever the form, living heartfully is the result of choosing to bring our spiritual practice into the whole of our lives.

Living heartfully is the result of choosing to bring our spiritual practice into the whole of our lives.

When we are blessed with a mutually loving and supportive partnership, we discover a multitude of opportunities to practice mindfulness and heartfulness. I recall the shift in my awareness after making a commitment to my relationship with my husband. Just as I had made a promise to myself to approach the difficult circumstances in my own life with as much openness to learning and growing as I could muster, I was now promising to do the same with him. It was no longer acceptable for me to shut down my openness to self-examination or turn off my compassion when problems arose. Our relationship was now included in what I considered to be sacred practice. Stories of couples who live out their commitments by meditating together daily, creating ritual around their sharing and listening to one another, and reaffirming their vows each morning offer much-needed models of what spirit-infused relationships can be. In them we find examples of how we can support each other in our spiritual practices and remind one another of the "calls to awakening" that we have heard.

In addition to serving as vehicles for spiritual practice, relationships may also be the source of what has been described as a spiritual experience—feeling connected to the moment. When we touch another person's heart, our own heart is touched, creating a transcendent feeling of oneness. It is as if we are united with the other person and through this union are also connected with God. Similarly, this phenomenon is often described to express the power of community. When people come together in a group, something emerges that is more potent than the sum of the group's members. The power of community can take on a magic of its own. The experience of being part of something that is larger than any one of us can be sacred.

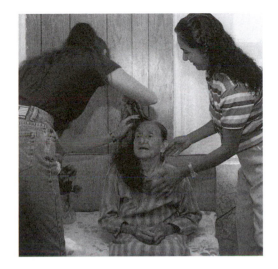

A traditional story illustrates the nourishing power of community. Beings suffering the torments of hell were compelled to attempt to feed themselves using spoons with handles longer than the reach of their arms. Bringing the spoons to their own mouths was impossible. These poor souls experienced searing anger and frustration, in addition to their hunger. At the same time, beings in a heavenly realm had been given the same long spoons. However, there no one went hungry, for these more fortunate souls had discovered that they could use the spoons to feed one another.

This spirit of cooperation and its power to alleviate suffering are central to the attraction we feel toward belonging, and indeed the story implies that this ability to look beyond one's own needs is a blessing. It is ironic, then, that in our culture of material abundance, this sense of blessedness is often scarce or missing entirely. Feelings of loneliness and isolation are almost epidemic. Perhaps because we are such a mobile society, fewer and fewer people report living lives bound by the thread of familiar places and people. I experienced this phenomenon in my own life after I moved from a smaller town to a large city. I was struck by the degree of disconnection I could observe even while walking down the street, and I could appreciate its isolating effect as I struggled to create a sense of community for myself.

In many spiritual traditions, the presence of a community of fellows devoted to pursuing a spiritual path is encouraged. In both East and West, monastic orders were founded to provide a place away from the usual concerns of the world and a means to honor—and be enriched by—a shared sense of vision. The power of these communities lies in their ability to bring members back to their intention to follow a discipline, by providing them with support, nourishment, and resistance against the currents of society that can throw them off center. Secular "intentional communities" have also flourished from time to time. The communes of the 1960s are a particularly well-known example of this tendency for a group of like-minded individuals to gather together in community to forge a life based on common principles.

Developing healthy communities, whether secular or spiritual, is more easily said than done. Especially in today's world, where fewer and fewer of us have experienced the sort of traditional social structures that our ancestors knew, with all of their benefits and obligations, it is difficult to find living examples of the ties that we are seeking. The same challenges apply to relationships in general. Most of us do not receive any type of education in how to go about developing a healthy spirit of tolerance and commitment to a larger whole. Those of us who are fortunate to be born into generous and loving families have opportunities to observe healthy relationships in action. Others may feel that it is necessary to unlearn the dysfunctional patterns of our families of origin, without any clear positive models to emulate.

While there are always circumstances beyond our control, it is helpful to consider ways in which we can actively participate in cultivating the type of social support that we desire and need. Just as growing a garden requires that we begin by weeding out

Especially in today's world, . . . it is difficult to find living examples of the ties that we are seeking.

unwanted plants and pests, it is sometimes appropriate to make decisions about the types of relationships that we do and do not want. This may require saying no to some community involvements or setting limits in certain friendships. It may also require that we leave intimate relationships that are unsupportive or toxic to our well-being. These acts allow us to create space and energy for the forms of companionship that we are seeking. If we can hold an image of the qualities that we want in our partners, friends, and community groups, we can begin directing our efforts toward cultivating relationships that touch us on all levels of our being.

Integrative Practices

Some of the most sacred moments of our lives are those spent in relationships. In the end, giving and receiving love from others is a fundamental quality of life.

Honoring Others

Close your eyes and imagine bowing to another person and offering the words, "I honor the light within you," as a greeting. You may want to begin by envisioning a person for whom you feel love. Now try this greeting once again, but this time imagine that you are bowing to someone who is neutral to you.

Then see what it feels like to imagine this interaction with someone with whom you have been angry. Try to carry the essence of this greeting with you as you go through your day, internally thinking these words and offering the intention of bowing to each person you encounter.

The Garden of Relationships

     Consider the relationships currently in your life. Are there any relationships that you feel you need to change so that they are more supportive to you? Are there any relationships in which you feel drawn to extend yourself more fully?

Befriending the Earth

A PERSONAL ODYSSEY
Diane Melvin

The dance of relationship also applies to our deep connection to the earth and everything around us.

Although we may have difficulty recognizing it, each human being feels a particular calling. I suppose that I have been fortunate, in that I clearly feel that my purpose on this planet is to help heal our earth and make the world a more peaceful and loving place to be. For this reason, I feel great sorrow in the depths of my soul when I witness environmental degradation. When I walk through a clearing for a new development, my tears fill the deer tracks imprinted in the new mud. I mourn the loss of life as the bulldozers tear into the wildness. I wonder why we have to be so wasteful, so caught up on our greed and self-importance that we constantly insist on having something new instead of reusing what we already have.

It is often very difficult to encourage environmental awareness because it goes against the current social fabric. While I sometimes feel discouraged, something motivates me to work harder to create a more peaceful world in which human beings are able to respect the needs of other creatures. I have discovered that I turn to nature for the strength and endurance necessary to continue in this important and healing work.

It is a deep spiritual connection with nature that sustains me. Nothing is more healing for me than to head into nature. I may walk, sit quietly under a tree or at the edge of a marsh, and listen. After quieting the chatter inside my mind, I can clearly hear the messages from the depths of my soul dancing on the wind around me. I feel surrounded by and filled with Spirit. Nothing is as effective in bringing clarity and wisdom to my mind and peace to my soul. I connect with the plants and animals around me on an intimate level. I pray to understand the wisdom that they hold and the lessons that they have to teach me. Watching the ants laboriously climbing up a rough tree bark carrying loads larger than they are gives me patience and perseverance.

The wisdom of nature is everywhere. As I overturn a rotting log, I watch the slugs, beetles, and worms transform the tree it once was into soil. This nutrient-rich soil provides the seedlings springing up around the old tree with a lush place to grow. So the cycle of life continues. Quiet observation of the natural world teaches me not to fear death but to accept it as another phase in the cycle of life. During such reflective moments I experience the cycles of nature as a circle that has no end.

Watching the clouds slowly rolling across the sky or the rays of sunshine streaming through the clouds reminds me of the beauty and enormity of Divinity. When I see such beauty in the sky around me, my perspective instantly shifts. Instead of being consumed by the immediate concerns of the moment—work, errands, mothering—I am suddenly aware of a much larger picture. Watching the clouds reminds me of what is really important and how my day-to-day concerns and activities fit into the larger pattern. Seeing this, I can continue my day, filled with peace and renewed purpose.

There are times in my life when I feel more connected with nature than others. When I have less time to be in nature, I not only feel cut off from the natural world but from Spirit and my inner self. Then I must struggle to remain grounded and centered. At times like this, it often seems easier to get caught up in the worries and concerns of the moment. Acting from my deeper life's purpose and true goals seems too difficult. It is overwhelming to work full-time, be a single mother, and just try to get the basics accomplished each day. Yet when I do make time to walk in the woods the rewards are immediate and abundant.

I gain helpful insights from my meditation time in nature. This is especially true when I go into the forest. I sense the wisdom found in the old trees around me. As I hug them I imagine all that they have seen in their lifetime. Being in the forest is like sitting surrounded by giant, wise old sages. The wisdom is there, but we often seem to have lost the ability to perceive it. To become attuned to this wisdom it is beneficial to become like the trees. They are so big and tall and strong. Firmly rooted in the soil, their trunks are flexible enough to allow the branches to blow in the wind. I, too, try to stay firmly rooted in my truth and my inner knowing while remaining flexible enough to withstand the winds of chaos that often blow around me.

Recalling such images when I am going about my daily business helps me stay grounded in what I understand to be true and real. Reliving such an experience helps keep in the forefront of my mind my larger life's purpose of working toward global peace and healing, even as I struggle to keep my family fed, housed, and clothed. My relationship to nature helps me nurture all of my other relationships—to friends, loved ones, my work, and all that is around me on this earth.

CHAPTER 6

Sharing the Harvest

Ripening

PAULA W. JAMISON

The practices described in the preceding chapters help us cultivate the seeds of awakening so that they may fully ripen. As we plant and patiently tend them, it becomes clear that each small grain has the power to blossom into great beauty. Yet while seeds and gardens have much to teach us about our own capacity for growth, there comes a time when we must envision our lives in our own way. Responding to the images that touch us, we discover the peculiar vantage point on the inner life that is ours alone.

Bringing our inner lives into outer form is one fruit of our efforts, born of experience and grace. Slowly we learn to approach relationships differently, or step by step we find a way to honor our commitment to integrate a healthier way of being into our

It is our willingness to be transformed that makes us into true pilgrims, seeking both the beauties of the world and what lies beneath appearances.

lives. We stick our necks out and with whatever grace we can muster attempt to hold our vision, even as we allow the world to teach us. When we are open to new relationships and learning, we experience life more fully than ever before.

In this sense, to tend the seeds of our awakening is to enter the mystery, for we must learn to live with our fears as well as our joys. It is our willingness to be transformed that makes us into true pilgrims, seeking both the beauties of the world and what lies beneath appearances. While each of our journeys is unique, we are often granted a sense of kinship that arises from recognizing our connection with the deepest core of our being.

As we experience this inner transformation, our priorities and sense of ourselves undergo a shift. Our everyday actions and relationships as well as our work in the world reflect these changes. Nurturing a growing vision of authenticity and wholeness in our work is one way of expressing a newly-felt connection with the larger world. Or we may find ourselves drawn to pondering or re-examining our gifts, finding support in the practices of contemplation and discernment. We may choose to devote more time and energy to serving others or realize that we have been giving too much of ourselves "away" and must honor our own needs. We discover forgiveness and find compassion for ourselves and others. Our harvest, then, is also a time for sharing the abundance. As we offer our gifts to the world, we are enriched and changed, as the cycle of growth continues.

The Way of Work

PAULA W. JAMISON

There comes a point when we want to test our budding insights by living in a new way. This may take the form of cooking healthy foods for our families, beginning an exercise program, or inviting our partner into a deeper level of dialogue than we had previously experienced. We may also discover, much to our dismay, that what once were vague rumblings of dissatisfaction about our job or marriage have now reached such a pitch that we feel compelled to take action, even if we do not know how to proceed. It is as if we are responding to an intuitive sense that tells us that no amount of personal exploration will carry us very far if we are not prepared to put our ideas and feelings "to work" in our everyday, ordinary lives. Something urges us to grapple with the question of how to live in wholeness and integrity in the world of people, things, and large institutional structures.

For most human beings, work is a necessity. Its omnipresence inspires passion, boredom, or outright aversion. For these and other reasons work has often been regarded as central to the path of inner development. The Christian tradition, as embodied in Benedictine monasticism, emphasizes the role that regular, often monotonous, and sometimes backbreaking work has in shaping the inner life of those who submit willingly to its demands. In India, Hinduism speaks of *seva*, or service, as a key component of a spiritual path in which practitioners express their gratitude for the bounties of life by selflessly serving others. These yogic traditions tell us that "karma yoga," or the yoga of action, is as valid a path to spiritual realization as practices with a more inward focus, such as meditation.

Intuitively we understand that work connects us with the larger community, offering us a "place" in a complex world.

Buddhism is even more specific, for one of the recommendations given in the most basic teaching known as the Eightfold Path is that of "right livelihood." To Buddhists, engaging in a form of livelihood not based on the taking of life or the exploitation of other beings is a fundamental way to liberation. Today many authors in the West have focused on bringing deepened awareness and understanding to work in the contemporary world as well.

Intuitively we understand that work connects us with the larger community, offering us roles and a "place" in a complex world. Yet many times, when we find ourselves face-to-face with this community—often in the form of large institutional structures that seem to have little concern for the individual—we end up feeling frustrated and disconnected. At such times our work "out there" seems alienating, and the financial rewards or the feeling of independence it gives us may not be enough to keep despair at bay. We try to live out our ideals and may become discouraged or feel isolated when others do not seem to share our concerns. However, this dissatisfaction can bring the potential for insight as Ellen's story reveals.

A young nurse named Ellen had taken her first job at a busy hospital. Frustrated with the impersonality of conventional high tech medical care, she began studying alternative treatments that emphasized more contact with the patient. She felt disheartened by the scorn her colleagues heaped upon "woo-woo healers." Yet because of her inexperience, she wanted to prove herself and thus felt unable to talk with them about her true interests. Isolated and torn in two, she struggled to hide an increasingly important dimension of her view of herself as a nurse and healer. One day, after several months of wondering whether she had chosen the right field, Ellen was struggling to keep her calm with one of her patients, an elderly woman with a severe degenerative form of arthritis. The older woman was often snappish and difficult, and this day was no exception. As Ellen was about to leave, the women brusquely called her back and said: "You know, the problem with you is that you think you're here to help me. Well, maybe yes and maybe no. But how can you know what's possible unless you stop fussing about how things *should* be and pay more attention to how they are?"

Later Ellen said that the woman's words, though startling, made more and more sense. "I didn't get all romantic about it," she said. "That patient continued to be a challenge. But her words helped me remember something important. In my excitement about bringing what I had into the world, I'd forgotten that I was also there to pay attention and learn from others."

Things did not get magically easier for Ellen, but from that day forward she found that she had a way of putting her frustrations into perspective. She began to discover that her work was an important way of entering into dialogue with the world. In this dialogue, she was often surprised and even uncomfortable by what she learned. Her sense of herself as a caring professional attentive to the needs of others was often challenged, for example, when she found that she was too preoccupied or exhausted to truly attend to a patient or co-worker. Yet when she listened to her exhaustion instead of shutting it out, it reminded her that she was doing too much. Before she could take care of anyone else, she needed to take care of herself.

Our work is a means of sharing the fruits of our inner harvest with others. For Ellen, work was a place where she hoped to relate to the world by offering something of herself for the larger good. It took courage and a continued willingness to pay attention for her to move beyond feeling trapped by structures and relationships that had been in place long before her arrival. Ellen's need to extend herself to others came from her heartfelt desire to be of service and share her growing wisdom. This way of looking at work exerts great power and offers the possibility of seeing ourselves as belonging to something greater than ourselves.

Yet when we focus primarily on our gifts we often forget about our part, as givers, in the larger exchange.

Yet when we focus primarily on our gifts we often forget about our part, as givers, in the larger exchange. At such times we run the risk of so closely identifying with what we have to offer that any hint of rejection or incomprehension wounds us deeply. We forget that as givers, we are also called upon to receive—and that what we receive may not be what we asked for. Our work, after all, is a conversation with the world. When we singlemindedly attend only to what we have to say, we miss the richness of the exchange. When we are open to what our work has to tell us, our sense of isolation drops away, and we experience the give-and-take of true relationship.

How, then, can we bring our newly awakened sense of wholeness into our work without feeling cut off or overwhelmed? While it is important to bring our outer lives into alignment with our inner awareness, it is vital to recognize that changing the *form* of our work will not serve us for long unless on some level we agree to let ourselves be changed as well. For work is a form of exchange not only in the economic sense, but psychically and socially as well. Indeed, we offer our time and skills in exchange for money or other results; but on all levels we also offer ourselves up to be *changed* by what we do.

When we are able to bring our full attention and awareness to our work as a way of meeting and being transformed by the world, we no longer focus solely on our own gifts and the needs they may represent for us—to be loved, accepted, or admired. What work teaches us, if we allow it, is how to bring what we have to share to the world and truly release it. When we approach work as an act of giving we come to realize that to give fully and from the heart is to allow what we have loved and created to go forth. And just as we can only breathe in new life and oxygen after we have exhaled, we are only truly open to receive the gifts the world has to offer us when we have released what we have brought with us and let it go.

What work teaches us, if we allow it, is how to bring what we have to share to the world and truly release it.

Seeing what we have to contribute in this way broadens the lens with which we view even a routine job or a work setting that may not reflect our values. When we are able to reduce the number of strings attached to our gifts and simply offer them up, we approach our relationship to work in a newfound spirit of lightness. Giving and receiving take on a new meaning.

❧

Integrative Practices

Bringing our work lives into harmony with our deepest selves is a crucial step on the path toward wholeness.

Work as Teacher

There is an old saying that a good tool teaches the craftsman how to use it. In other words, the actual shape and heft of the object will guide the hand, literally instructing the worker in its proper use. On a more subtle level, the work we do has much to teach us, not only about our selves but about how to be more fully in the world.

Reflect upon the gifts that your work is offering you right now. What are the joys you experience? What are the lessons you have been struggling to learn?

Finding the Healer Within

It has been said that when it comes to offering healing to others, whether in the formal role as healer or in any relationship, who we *are* is as important as what we know or what skills we possess.

What are the qualities that you bring to being in relationship with others that can be healing? What essential aspects of yourself would you like to be able to bring into your interactions with others? How are you able to embody these qualities in the workplace or while carrying out your daily tasks, right now?

The Heart at Work

A PERSONAL ODYSSEY
K'Anna Burton

For me, work is a place where it is possible to move into a sense of harmony with the larger world around us. The actions we take as part of our work express our relationship to the living planet—and we can attempt to see and understand this relationship and treat it with honor if we so choose. Attending to our work in this way, seeing it as the opportunity to be in relationship, makes working an act filled with healing potential. It is our choice to find meaning, enrichment, or growth in the work we do.

A friend of mine, a single mother in need of money to support herself and her children, once took a job that was not in harmony with all her values. She found herself employed at a large educational and medical institution. She knew this was a "good job" financially and that she needed to be there for at least a few years. So, she went looking for how she could bring her heart, her whole authentic self to this job. She knew that if she could do this, she would be able to find meaning, enrichment, and growth. She chose to bring the best she had in any moment to the young medical students, the actual people with whom she had the most direct contact.

She often spoke fondly of this or that "young doc." She made extra efforts to *be there* for them, mindful and attentive to their educational and sometimes personal needs. Working with them, she found "right livelihood" and a place of right relationship to the work she was choosing to do at that time. She continued to be challenged by some co-workers, by her administrative supervisors, and even the lack of warmth in her work surroundings. And even so, she loved the part of her job that allowed her to find heart and meaning.

Offering Our Gifts to the World

KAREN HORNEFFER-GINTER

Once we have experienced a moment of awakening to the connection between ourselves and the world around us, it is not uncommon to feel a pull toward helping others. This may be motivated by our own experience of healing, or come from a deep sense of gratitude for what we have in our lives. Whatever the initial motivation, when we consider serving others we embark on a journey of transforming our intentions into action. As we begin the process of deciding what form our efforts will take, we are faced with several exciting and challenging questions.

First, we must consider how to go about helping others. Should we carry out our passion through a professional role, such as teacher, counselor, nurse, minister, doctor, or activist? Or does it feel more fitting to be healing to others in more informal ways, such as in our daily relationships with family, friends, and co-workers? While choosing a form for our helping may be an easy task for some, for others the way is far from simple. Sometimes we feel that we have nothing to offer, or that what we have is insufficient. We may feel that we have to give something extraordinary and develop talents that we do not currently possess. We may doubt our ability to realize our dreams and be too easily reminded of life experiences that make us question our potential to be effective. Sometimes, however, the process of getting in touch with our insecurities and vulnerability helps us discover what we bring to the world. It may be that the very experiences that contributed to these feelings of doubt or emptiness may also lead to deepened awareness, sensitivity, and kindness—the root of our gifts to others.

The process of naming our gift does not require birthing some new quality within us but rather giving expression to what is already at the core of who we are.

The process of naming our gift does not require birthing some new quality within us but rather giving expression to what is already at the core of who we are. It may also be a matter of recognizing that what we already do serves others—including such everyday actions as preparing meals, fixing things, or sharing a kind word. In order to identify these qualities and to become aware of our passion, reflection and contemplation are needed, as well as a willingness to openly look at the lives we already lead.

I recall a period when I was trying to discover how my desire to be of service could be of use to the world. I initially approached the task by looking outside of myself: I was identifying available opportunities and looking for a niche. While driving home one night in the rain I made a discovery. Watching the rain run down the windshield I noticed that the light from the street lamps was making the raindrops form crosses. The stream of light created between each bulb seemed to be about one-third as long as the stream of light that ran vertically, below and above each lamp.

Staring at these forms reminded me that I should spend more time *deepening* my relationship to myself by being open to the inward call of what my work was to be about. I laughed as I realized that even the proportions seemed appropriate—to spend three times as much effort in my inward contemplation of how to serve others as I do in my external searching or reaching out into the world. From this perspective, we first give birth to our gift from the inside, as we identify what we have to offer. Only then do we look outward to see how it can fit into the world.

While naming our gift can be a powerful moment in and of itself, it also signifies the beginning of a process of keeping our passion alive. Just as planted seeds require ongoing care to grow, so too do our visions of being of service. It can be daunting just to consider the number of people and causes deserving attention. Bombarded with images of suffering, we may be overwhelmed and struggle to keep our hearts open. As we contemplate the world's needs, from starving children and endangered species to political injustices, it is no wonder that our gifts may suddenly seem to pale in comparison to the tasks required. In such moments, it is useful to have a realistic view of our role.

At these times it is helpful to step back and see ourselves— and our gifts—as unique elements that combine with myriads of others to form the beauty of the natural world. When we look out at the trees and flowers, the richness of the tapestry before us comes from the variety of species that together make up our earth. When we are able to recognize our part in the greater whole, it becomes easier to recall that our role is not to heal the world but to offer opportunities for healing to those with whom we have contact.

Another means of keeping our passion alive is to continually spark our enthusiasm for the work that we do by remembering *why* we are doing what we are doing. I think of the times in my work as a psychologist that I have lost touch with the potential for healing within my role. At such moments it becomes easy to go through the motions at work, especially when I am feeling tired or burdened. Then it is necessary to renew my conscious intention to serve others by reawakening to what excites me. This may take the form of learning new things, having contact with others, or allowing myself the time to attend to my own needs. Such activities are essential not only to individuals whose work has placed them in the role of helper or healer but to anyone who wishes to continue approaching his or her work in a fresh and meaningful way.

Whatever our work, we each must find a balance between helping others and taking care of ourselves. There is a common human tendency to take our efforts to extremes. On the one hand, a shortcoming of the "self-improvement" surge in the 1980s was that people began to focus intensely on their personal issues, to the exclusion of considering the needs of others. Self-care does not mean self-absorption. On the other hand, the decision to embark on the journey of being of service to others can bring a similarly myopic illusion that it is *always* best to be in the role of giver or provider. It is ironic that the same people who can be so astute at meeting the needs of others can be so slow to respond to the cries of their own hearts, bodies, or spirits. Examples of burned out or disillusioned helpers serve as important reminders of the inherent necessity for balance.

Just as the cycles of nature are punctuated by the ebb and flow of life's currents, we too have our own individual rhythms. Women have long been reminded of the connection between their monthly cycles and those of the moon, with its waxing and waning. But all of us would benefit from recalling the movement from the light of action into the darkness of contemplation and rest that governs the natural world. To expect ourselves to be like the sun, being "on" every day and able to constantly provide for others, is a denial of the fundamental rhythms of nature. When we

Our role is not to heal the world but to offer opportunities for healing to those with whom we have contact.

ignore these, we deny our need for rest, replenishment, and the inspiration that can be found only when we give ourselves time to slow down and listen.

Leading a life of awareness requires that we come to know our inner rhythms. How much can I give before I begin to feel resentful? What are the signs that tell me that I need to take time for myself? Do I feel it in my body or in my emotions? What activities allow me to "fill my cup" before I become depleted? Although the answers will vary at different points in our lives, it is essential that we remember to ask ourselves these questions.

Not only does this type of reflection help us develop a balance between our inner lives and outer work, it informs our service to others, making it the authentic expression of who we are. The question of how to integrate our sense of self and our care for others can be tricky. What will we bring to the role of healer? Are there parts of ourselves that we must leave behind? It may seem odd to think that people feel a need to leave behind parts of themselves as they step into roles of service, but this often happens, albeit unconsciously. We may feel that there is no room for our sense of humor when we are confronted with another's pain, or that expressing our own emotions is inappropriate in front of those we are helping. In training counselors, I have often seen students feel the need to adopt a different persona as they enter the room with a client. Suddenly their voices change, along with their whole demeanor. There is a sense that something has been left outside the room, and a stiffness fills the air.

If we cannot find a way to be ourselves, and adopt only the role and techniques of a healer, counselor, or teacher, for example, what we offer to others is incomplete. It could even be said that when it comes to serving others, *who we are* is as important as what we know or the skills we possess. Part of our challenge, then, is to consider how our service can be a full expression of who we are. How can we authentically share ourselves with others so that

When it comes to serving others, who we are is as important as what we know or the skills we possess.

we are truly present in our acts of service?

A final question worth considering is, What does it mean to serve others, to be a healer or helper? Even the form of the question is misleading, for it implies that some people offer service and others do not. This erroneous distinction may only serve to separate people from the naturalness of their need to extend themselves to others. It seems more accurate to acknowledge that we are all here to serve. We are all healers and helpers at some times and in certain ways. More importantly, the roles that we assume, whether as provider or receiver, are more illusory than real. Sometimes it is in our giving that we receive most deeply.

At this level of awareness we are reminded not to take our roles of healer, helper, physician, teacher, activist, or parent too seriously. The work, yes, should be taken to heart, but the role is nothing more than a form that we adopt to interact with others. Can we learn to give with a compassionate wisdom that does not force the other person to take on the role of receiver? Can we offer our care, skills, and presence in a manner that does not disempower those we serve?

Paradoxically, our ability to help without minimizing in any way the capacities of the people we serve runs parallel to our ability to fully accept the worthiness of what we have to offer. When we know our value within ourselves, there is no need to force others into acknowledging that we have given them anything. We merely need to be present to the grace of the moment. As we offer our gifts to the world, then, we engage in the ongoing task of learning to honor what we have to bring to others. As Marriane Williamson notes, "As we let our own light shine, we give other people permission to do the same; as we're liberated from our own fear, our presence automatically liberates others." When we serve others out of our own joy of living and self-acceptance, we offer them not only an extension of ourselves but a reminder that they too have unique gifts to contribute to the world.

As we offer our gifts to the world, then, we engage in the ongoing task of learning to honor what we have to bring to others.

❧

Integrative Practices

The path of service need not take the form of a specific job or career. What is important is that the desire to serve be grounded in your own capacity to be joyful and to find inner nourishment both in and outside of your work.

Finding Joy

Consider the idea, "Our calling is where our greatest joy meets the world's greatest need." Write down some thoughts about what it is that brings you joy. How does joy *feel?* What does joy look like? Reflect on any sensations or images that come to you.

Finding Balance

Take a few moments to reflect upon what the optimal balance is for you between serving others and taking care of yourself. Do you recall an experience in which you overextended yourself to others and felt burned out?

What are the cues that alert you that you need to rest, and what type of activities replenish you? Note any insights that arise concerning this rhythm in your life.

Fruits of the Harvest: Compassion

PAULA W. JAMISON

Teachers of all the great wisdom traditions emphasize that the first fruits of the harvest of awareness include compassion, gratitude, and joy. Compassion holds a special place among the three. The journey of awakening opens our hearts and makes them tender, taking us beyond the acknowledgment of our own suffering and isolation to a sense of kinship with our fellow beings. This experience of connection with others makes us alive to their pain, all the while making our hearts resonate with their joy. We feel in harmony with a greater whole, touched by the beauties of the world and awed by the preciousness of all life.

As we look upon our own lives with opened hearts, we also

are able to see the gifts that came to us beneath all the suffering and pain we have experienced. We come to understand that once painful choices have not only led to our learning to live with loss but also have made room for new sources of joy. When we discover that we are grateful for the lessons of our lives, it is not because we are able to look back and simply say, "All was good, because some good has come of it." To do so would be to ignore our pain—and in doing so, perhaps make us blind to the suffering of others. Our gratitude is a way of honoring the wholeness of our lives, shadows as well as sunlight.

Indeed, the fruits of our harvest include joy and sorrow, delight and frustration, the awareness of breathtaking inequities as well as awe-inspiring courage. When we are able to acknowledge, even embrace, our woundedness, our incompleteness, we have a choice, however elusive and unattainable it may seem. We may remain fixated on our own hurt, focusing on ourselves alone, or we may accept our flawed humanity and extend this practice of compassion to other beings as well. When we do so, we move out of our sense of isolation into a new connection with others. We become alive to the world.

Still, for most of us, such moments of recognition are fleeting and resist all of our efforts to grasp them. One way to know the abiding gratitude and joy described in the spiritual traditions is to learn the art of forgiveness. By forgiving those who have wronged us, we bring healing not only to a specific relationship. We help restore our sense of place in the human family. By forgiving ourselves (and this is especially important in cases where we find it impossible to forgive others), we bring the balm of forgiveness deep into our own hearts. There we know the peace of letting go.

Practicing the art of forgiveness helps us to remain faithful to our awakening sense of wholeness, even as we inevitably continue to suffer pain, sorrow, and disappointment. Our need to

By forgiving those who have wronged us, . . . [w]e help restore our sense of place in the human family.

find healing through forgiveness leads us to reach out to others, just as it encourages us to be patient with ourselves and all our failings. Nourished by the work of forgiveness, compassion can become our steadfast companion, bestowing upon us gratitude and joy or teaching us trust when gratitude and joy have become distant and unattainable. When we feel isolated or rebuffed and the desire to share the fruits of our inner harvest with others is stilled, the power of compassion remains, giving us courage to proceed on our journey with open hearts.

Integrative Practices

True compassion comes from a deep experiential understanding of our commonality with others and from the acceptance of our own exquisitely flawed humanity.

Touching Our Compassionate Hearts

The following meditation is based on the Buddhist practice known as "loving kindness." Find a quiet place where you will be undistrubed.

Take a comfortable position, allowing the body to relax. Feel the breath slowly deepen and become more regular. Simply be with the ebbing and flowing of the breath. Then visualize someone you hold dear. Imagine this person sitting across from you, looking at you with tenderness. Say to this person in your mind, "May you find happiness. May you be free from suffering. May you find peace." Sit with the feelings that arise at this moment, gradually turning your attention once again to the breath.

Then bring to mind someone you know less well and feel neutral about. Imagine this person sitting across from you, looking tenderly at you. Say to this person in your mind, "May you find happiness. May you be free from suffering. May you find peace." Sit with the feelings that arise.

Last, hold an image of yourself in your mind, perhaps as a young child or during a time of difficulty in your life. Imagine that she or he is sitting across from you, looking tenderly at you. Say to this person in your mind, "May you find happiness. May you be free from suffering. May you find peace." Notice any feelings or images that arise at this moment and sit with them quietly. Return your awareness to the breath and spend a few more moments in this relaxed posture. Gradually return your attention to the room around you.

Gratitude and Giving

Take a moment to come into awareness of what your body feels like right now. Over the next few breaths, bring to mind something—either great or small—for which you are grateful. As you inhale, bring this feeling of gratitude into your body. On the exhalation extend this feeling of gratitude to the entire world around you. How does it feel when you do this?

Forgiveness
A PERSONAL ODYSSEY

FRITZ MACDONALD

Discovering our true nature is a painstaking process. As we gradually become clearer about who we are, we are often called upon to respond to the perceptions of others, which at times seem to imprison us in an old, discarded self. At moments like this, relating to those around us is one of the great challenges of the transformative journey.

How forgiveness and gratitude generate healing, allowing the spirit to enter into our daily lives, is a mystery. In the case of my own family I struggled angrily for years to convince them that I was not the seventeen-year-old they all remembered but a doctor of philosophy and a university professor. As a teenager I had aspired to become a professional singer. I realize now that this aspiration came in large part from the influence of my family. Whenever we gathered for celebrations there was always music, and I was inevitably called upon to sing a few songs. There was never a more appreciative audience nor a more loving one.

As time passed and I approached thirty years of age, it became increasingly clear to me that a stable career in singing was not going to materialize. There were simply better singers around with greater self-confidence. In 1975, my wife and I returned to the United States from Germany, where I had been struggling for success as an opera singer. I entered graduate school to begin a second career. With a master's degree in social work, and later a Ph.D., I naturally assumed that my family would recognize and praise my accomplishments. I was hoping that they at least would hint that I had more than made up for my failure as a singer. Nothing of the kind transpired.

At every Christmas or Thanksgiving that I returned to western New York with my wife and children to visit my parents, aunts, uncles, and cousins, hardly a question was asked about my work and accomplishments. Instead the requests came to sing a "couple of good old songs"—as if I had never been other than that seventeen-year-old who sang with abandon for his family's pleasure. The passage of time seemed suspended. My present life, with its challenges and satisfactions, did not seem to exist for the people I loved.

At first this was difficult, for in some ways I blamed them for giving me unrealistic notions about my singing abilities. Couldn't they understand the sense of failure I had experienced because of their inaccurate perceptions? Couldn't they respect my feelings of grief and loss and let me be rather than continually remind me of a failed career? For some years, I stopped going home altogether. Yet gradually, as I saw my aunts and uncles become increasingly frail, it began to dawn on me that time spent with them was a precious gift.

The last time I was with my two aunts and one of my uncles, I sang a song they knew. We wept together in a kind of epiphany of love. As I awakened to the realization that these people loved me dearly, I understood at last how they had always conveyed acceptance and affirmation. My heart opened, and I was able to sing again for them with joy and abandon. The attachment to my own strivings for success in the larger world—along with the subsequent grief, anger, and resentment I had been experiencing for all those years around the act of singing—dropped away. Later that same year, when my oldest aunt died suddenly, my cousins called on me to sing the mass at her funeral and a few songs for the family. With gratitude, I accepted the invitation.

CHAPTER 7

Conclusion

Coming Home to Simplicity

MOLLY VASS-LEHMAN AND PAULA W. JAMISON

'Tis the gift to be simple,
  'Tis the gift to be free,
  'Tis the gift to come down
  Where we ought to be . . .

        Shaker Hymn

Through the cycles and seasons of our lives, as we continue to grow in awareness, we begin to feel more at home in the world. We begin to appreciate and accept who we are. While not condoning our faults and lapses, we come to a place of forgiveness and self-acceptance. We no longer strive to be someone else. The journey to this place of authenticity is not straightforward or smooth. Indeed, it is a great gift to be able to see—and trust—the wholeness of the process. We move from periods of joyful expansion into a dark night of the soul. We seem to reap the harvest of the sustained practice of attention and compassion and come to know ourselves in a new and more forgiving light, only to forget and return to what we thought were old, discarded ways. We grow. We rest. We find stillness. We leap into life with joy. We withdraw. We suffer and we experience great delight. Yet deep within is a place of understanding, and to find this place is to come home.

Coming home, we meet what is true, familiar, and at the root of our being. In this place we experience a glimmer of recognition that affirms our life and reveals a longed-for truth. A lifetime of searching takes on new meaning, as the fragments are knit into a whole. It is as if we have found the missing piece to a jigsaw puzzle that reveals the full picture. At such times, we are gifted with true sight, the vision that encompasses and gives value to our place in the universe. Coming home in this way has a profound impact on our outer lives as well. We respond by making room for this place of inner being—our inner home—in our actions and relationships.

Living in this way we express our faithfulness to ourselves. Such loyalty is not the result of steadfastly cultivating concepts of who we are and how we ought to be. Instead it arises when we are truly present and open to all that life has to give and take from us. It is marked by the acceptance that is born of understanding and true attunement with the ways of the universe. When we find this harmony we are also drawn into a deeper appreciation of the natural rhythms of growth, decay, and rebirth.

We learn to approach our own struggles in a spirit of understanding and forgiveness. Not all our good intentions—for ourselves or others—bear fruit. If conditions are not right, the seeds we have sown fade and die. Yet even in dying they decompose and give rise to new forms of life. Our process of learning and

Letting go is an art that we never perfect yet have countless opportunities to practice.

forgetting, welcoming and letting go, obeys these fundamental laws, but we are often so in love with our ideas of how we and things "ought" to be that we forget we are part of a larger pattern. Attunement to the overarching whole means that we are constantly refining our capacity to let go.

Letting go is an art that we never perfect yet have countless opportunities to practice. As we learn to let go, we are invited to open into what awaits us in the next, always unknowable, moment. We are invited to be surprised. Sometimes we cannot let go because we have an inflated sense of the importance of our own mortality. As we grow older and see our lives as increasingly finite, we may be driven to do more, have more, and experience more. When we fail to see beyond ourselves, to feel through every fiber of our being that we are part of a larger order of eternal life, we may be driven to attempt to do it all now. This sense of urgency is some-

times acute among people near the end of the lives when they have projects to complete. Even so, the reality is that we all eventually will have to let go of what has not been accomplished—and of life itself. No matter who we are or how important our work, a time will come when others will take our places, continuing our work or not as they see fit.

It takes deep faith and trust to try not to assume more than our part in the larger mosaic of life. When we feel that we are responsible for more than our share, it is as easy to miss living in the present moment as it is when we are focused on the future or obsessed with the past. Rest, balanced with awareness, gives rise to a true "responsiveness" to life and our own hearts, which is far removed from the burden of responsibility that is in truth the shell of a sense of self-importance. When we feel that our lives belong to an endless flow, we are more able to relax. Letting go of our self-importance makes it possible for the light within us to shine into the world.

These moments of realization are not static. Our awareness of belonging waxes and wanes. At the same time, our growing capacity for discernment may lead us to be disappointed in aspects of ourselves that we once had unthinkingly accepted. We may find ourselves regretting previous decisions, or feeling that we have wasted portions of our lives. Bringing the image of the garden to mind helps us remember, however, that nothing is ever truly lost. Indeed, it is possible and likely that certain past actions and decisions are the source of mourning. Yet the seed that does not sprout nourishes the ground out of which other plants will grow, while weeds and pests make it possible for the gardener to learn patience and careful discernment. At the same time, overabundant seeds must be culled, to make room for those plants which are left to grow, teaching us—once again—the need for letting go to make room for the unknown that will come next.

Despite the multiplicity and abundance of our experiences, and our endless struggles to live fully and with integrity in our wholeness, in the end the pattern is a simple one. When we can allow ourselves simply to be, to attend to the stirrings of the inner and outer worlds, sometimes a new sense of clarity emerges. It is not an easy task to appreciate or even apprehend such simplicity. Perhaps, as the words to the old Shaker tune have it, simplicity is a gift. Yet it is a gift granted through our attention and kept only at the cost of steady awareness.

Often we strive for ways to access the wisdom within us and recognize and embrace the wisdom of others. But to be able to discover, remember, and sustain the insights that come to us requires that we learn to pay attention consistently and nonjudgmentally. Living as we do, surrounded by distractions, it takes courage and hope to live our lives in wholeness and integrity. The following poem by Mark Nepo reminds us that what is essential is so simple and yet so difficult:

Letting go of our self-importance makes it possible for the light within us to shine into the world.

"Unearthed Again"

It starts out simple,
gets complicated and, by
burning what is not real,
gets simple again.

But it's never done.
No matter if we're tired,
spring comes and some undying
impulse needs to break ground.

It's the same with denial,
that winter of the heart. One day,
if blessed, the tulip coated with soil
is again a tulip,
and with an urgency we thought
we bequeathed, we must wake.

I think we would forget
all the ways to study in school
and just wait for this moment.

Those who wake are the students.
Those who stay awake are the teachers.

It's all as simple, as hard
as staring into ourselves, each other,
this moment
as we would into the sun
until we're blind
until we see.

As we learn to live in greater harmony and
awareness, we become attuned to the commonality
that underlies our sense of uniqueness. Separate and
yet at one with the world, we feel the rising and
falling of the breath. Moving in and out of stillness

we know great joy and grief, communion and isolation, all at once. Remembering, forgetting, we return over and over to this awareness of an inner longing to grow and follow the path we sometimes only seem to have chosen. When our whole being *knows,* we are touched with a clarity and sense of purpose that indeed shines a bright light upon the world. And when we are again called to darkness we withdraw and retreat, once again riding the rhythms of our being. Honoring and remembering, dancing and being danced, our spirit is awakened and takes us home.

Notes

References

Chapter 1

INTRODUCTION

David Whyte, *Where Many Rivers Meet* (Langley, WA: Many Rivers Press, 1996), p. 76.

Found in Richard Carlyon, *A Guide to the Gods: An Essential Guide to World Mythology* (New York: Quill Press, 1981), p. 376. Cited in an unpublished manuscript, by Mark Nepo.

Jacques Lusseyran, *And There Was Light* (Boston: Little, Brown and Co., 1963), pp. 16-17.

Helen M. Luke, *Such Stuff As Dreams Are Made On: The Autobiography and Journals of Helen M. Luke.* Journals edited by Barbara Mowat. (New York: Parabola Books, 2000), p. 2.

Chapter 2

RECAPTURING WONDER

Robert Lehman, Unpublished report (Kalamazoo, MI: The Fetzer Institue, 1999).

Mary Oliver, *New and Selected Poems* (Boston: Beacon Press, 1992), p. 94.

RECOVERY OF THE SENSES

Story taken from author files

J. Konrad Stettbacher, *Making Sense of Suffering: The Healing Confrontation with Your Own Past* (New York: Meridian, 1993), p. 13.

Dennis Linn, Sheila Fabricant Linn, and Matthew Linn, *Sleeping with Bread: Holding What Gives you Life* (Mahwah, NJ: Paulist Press, 1995), p. 1.

Story taken from author files

THE BODY AS GRACE

F. I. Kass, J. M. Oldham, and H. Pardes, eds. *The Columbia University College of Physicians and Surgeons Complete Home Guide to Mental Health* (New York: Henry Holt/Owl Books, 1995), p. 69.

Mark Nepo, "A Waterfall of Hands" (Unpublished manuscript), used with permission of the author.

LEARNING TO LISTEN WITHIN

Wendy Wright, "Passing Angels: The Arts of Spiritual Discernment," *Weavings*, vol. 10, no.6 (Nov/Dec 1995): 12.

Story taken from author files

Story taken from author files

Chapter 3

CONTEMPLATION

Natan Sharansky, *Fear No Evil,* translated by Stefani Hoffman (New York: Random House,1988).

REMEMBERING REST

Nikos Kazantzakis, *Zorba the Greek*, translated by Carl Wildman (New York: Simon and Schuster, 1953), pp. 120-121; cited in Jack Kornfield, *A Path With Heart* (New York: Bantam Doubleday Dell, 1993), p. 313.

Judith Lasater, *Relax and Renew: Restful Yoga for Stressful Times,* (Berkeley, CA: Rodmell Press, 1995), p. 5.

MINDFULNESS
Story taken from author files

RITUAL
Story taken from author files

Jeanne Achterberg, Barbara Dossey, and Leslie Kolkmeier, *Rituals of Healing: Using Imagery for Health and Wellness* (New York: Bantam Books, 1994), p. 3.

Chapter 4
EXPRESSION AND HEALING
Story taken from author files

LANGUAGES OF HEALING
James W. Pennebaker, *Opening Up: The Healing Power of Expressing Emotions,* revised edition (New York: Guilford Press, 1997).

J. M. Smyth, A.A. Stone, A. Hurewitz, and A. Kaell, "Effects of Writing about Stressful Experiences on Symptom Reduction in Patients with Asthma and Rheumatoid Arthritis," *Journal of the American Medical Association* 281 (1999): 1304-09.

ON KEEPING A JOURNAL
Deena Metzger, *Writing for Your Life: A Guide and Companion to the Inner Worlds* (San Francisco: Harper San Francisco,1992), p. 8.

A. J. Decasper, and M. J. Spence, "Prenatal Maternal Speech Influences Newborn's Perception of Speech Sounds." *Infant Behavior and Development* 9 (1986): 133-50.

RECLAIMING THE ARTIST WITHIN

Thomas Moore, *Care of the Soul: A Guide for Cultivating Depth and Sacredness in Everyday Life* (New York: Harper Perennial, 1994), p. 290.

Story taken from author files

Story taken from author files

SOUND, MUSIC, AND HEALING

Mark Nepo, "Where the HeartBeast Sings," *Sufi: A Journal of Sufism* 38 (Spring 1998): 22-23.

Don G. Cambell, *The Mozart Effect: Tapping the Power of Music to Heal the Body, Strengthen the Mind, and Unlock the Creative Spirit* (New York: Avon Books, 1997), pp. 64-69, 71, 191-92.

Jack Kornfield, *A Path With Heart: A Guide Through the Perils and Promises of Spiritual Life* (New York: Bantam Doubleday Dell, 1993), p. 334.

AWAKENING THROUGH MOVEMENT

Diane Mariechild, *The Inner Dance: A Guide to Spiritual and Psychological Unfolding* (Freedom, CA: The Crossing Press, 1987), p. 1.

Ellen Zachs, "The Body and Movement in Psychotherapy." Handout from a workshop entitled "Authentic Movement," San Diego, CA, 1990.

Story taken from author files

Chapter 5

RELATIONSHIP AND HEALING

Martin Buber, *I and Thou* (New York: Charles Scribner's Sons, 1958), pp. 3-4.

Carl Rogers, *A Way of Being* (New York: Houghton Mifflin, 1980), 14-17.

CONNECTING WITH OUR INNER SELVES

Richard C. Schwartz, *Internal Family Systems Therapy* (New York: The Guilford Press, 1995).

John Rowan, *Subpersonalities: The People Inside Us* (New York: Routledge, 1990).

Virginia Satir, *Your Many Faces: The First Step to Being Loved* (Millbrae, CA: Celestial Arts, 1978).

Walt Whitman, *Leaves of Grass* (New York: Doubleday Doran & Co, 1940), pp. 37-38.

Stephen Mitchell, *The Enlightened Heart* (New York: Harper and Row, 1989), p. 4.

Molly Young Brown, *The Unfolding Self: Psychosynthesis and Counseling* (Los Angeles: Psychosynthesis Press, 1983), pp. 11-12.

Stephen Mitchell, *The Enlightened Heart,* (New York: Harper and Row, 1989), p. 4.

Thich Nhat Hanh, talk at Plum Village, France, February 1996.

HONORING OTHERS

Dean Ornish, *Love and Survival: Pathways to Intimacy and Health* (New York: Harper Collins, 1998), Chapter 2.

David Spiegel, *Living Beyond Limits: New Hope and Help for Facing Life-Threatening Illness* (New York: Ballantine Books, 1993).

Starhawk, *The Spiral Dance* (New York: Harper Collins, 1989), p. 209.

Chapter 6
THE WAY OF WORK
Story taken from author files

OFFERING OUR GIFTS TO THE WORLD
Noted spiritual teacher and activist Ram Dass offers helpful advice about being of service in his book, *Compassion in Action* (New York: Bell Tower, 1992).

Marianne Williamson, *A Return to Love: Reflections on the Principles of "A Course In Miracles"* (New York: Harper Perennial, 1993), pp. 190-91.

FRUITS OF THE HARVEST: COMPASSION
Loving kindness meditation adapted from Stephen Levine, *Guided Meditations, Explorations and Healings* (New York: Anchor Books, 1991), pp. 29-32.

Chapter 7
COMING HOME TO SIMPLICITY
Edward D. Andrews, *The Gift to be Simple: Songs, Dances, and Rituals of the American Shakers* (New York: J. J. Augustin Publisher, 1940).

Mark Nepo, unpublished poem. With permission of the author.

Resources

The following is a brief list of "favorite" resources offered by each of the authors. By no means exhaustive, it is intended to offer further glimpses into the topics presented in the preceding chapters or to provide additional opportunities for practical exploration.

INTRODUCTION: AWAKENING

Muller, Wayne. *How Then Shall We Live? Four Simple Questions that Reveal the Beauty and Meaning of Our Lives.* New York: Bantam Books, 1996.

This book poses important questions that help to lead readers into a greater understanding of the meaning of their lives and encourages them to make conscious choices based on this knowledge.

Nepo, Mark. *The Book of Awakening: Having the Life You Want by Being Present to the Life You Have.* Berkeley, CA: Conair Press, 2000.

This is a guidebook of daily readings that offer support and companionship on the journey. It provides a guide to living with greater awareness and wholeness.

CONTEMPLATION

Palmer, Parker J. *Let Your Life Speak: Listening for the Voice of Vocation.* San Francisco: Jossey-Bass Books, 2000.

The author invites us to learn to listen to our inner truth and to have the courage to live based on this understanding. Through stories from his own life and the lives of others, he provides support for going deeper into the true meaning and purpose of our lives.

Cooper, David A. *Silence, Simplicity, and Solitude: A Guide for Spiritual Retreat.* New York: Bell Tower, 1992.

A wise and balanced introduction outlining the importance and practice of solitude in the world's major spiritual traditions. This book offers helpful suggestions for nurturing and supporting contemplative practices in modern life.

REMEMBERING REST

Muller, Wayne. *Sabbath: Restoring the Sacred Rhythm of Rest.* New York: Bantam Books, 1999.

This book helps bring an understanding to the importance of times of rest and renewal. It also provides ways to cultivate a sense of the sacred through stories, poems, and practices that can be incorporated into the daily rhythms of our lives.

Lasater, Judith. *Relax and Renew: Restful Yoga for Stressful Times.* Berkeley, CA: Rodmell Press, 1995.

This book can help individuals learn to listen to their bodies and to allow relaxation and renewal of energy through restful yoga practices. The insights and practices in this book can assist each individual in developing greater awareness of the relationship between body, mind, and spirit.

MINDFULNESS

Kabat-Zinn, Jon. *Wherever You Go, There You Are: Mindfulness Meditation in Everyday Life.* New York: Hyperion, 1994.

This is a simple and straightforward introduction to the practice of mindfulness. Kabat-Zinn illustrates ways to bring awareness and meditation into our lives to relieve stress, promote healing, and to awaken to a deeper way of being in the world.

Nhat Hanh, *Thich, Present Moment, Wonderful Moment.* Berkeley, CA: Parallax Press, 1990.

This is a small book giving a wide range of simple ways to bring mindfulness into everyday life. Practices are designed to help transform daily activities such as eating, talking on the phone, or washing yourself into mindfulness opportunities. This book is very practical rather than theoretical.

RITUAL

Achterberg, Jean, Dossey, Barbara, and Kolkmeier, Leslie. *Rituals of Healing: Using Imagery for Health and Wellness.* New York: Bantam Books, 1994.

Intended for individuals coping with physical or emotional "dis-ease" as well as those who wish to optimize their well-being, this book provides helpful information on how to create healing rituals. The authors discuss the research supporting the effectiveness of the body-mind connection created through the use of imagery, which can take the form of verbal descriptions or visual depictions.

Louden, Jennifer. *The Woman's Retreat Book: A Guide to Restoring, Rediscovering and Reawakening Your True Self—in a Moment, an Hour, a Day, or a Weekend.* San Francisco: Harper San Francisco, 1997.

While geared toward women, this book offers helpful suggestions on how to set apart sacred times and places for retreat and contemplation. The section on "opening ceremonies" is particularly helpful.

CREATIVITY

Diaz, Adriana. *Freeing the Creative Spirit: Drawing on the Power of Art to Tap the Magic and Wisdom Within.* San Francisco: Harper San Francisco, 1992.

This book is a hands-on guide to honoring the creative nature of the human spirit. Diaz includes two dozen exercises that guide the reader step-by step through blockages to being creative, exploring creativity as play, and using creativity for self-discovery.

Rogers, Natalie. *The Creative Connection: Expressive Arts as Healing.* Palo Alto, CA: Science and Behavior Books, 1993.

Rogers, daughter of psychologist Carl Rogers, offers ways to explore one's innate creativity in this inspiring book. She suggests that using all the senses and several creative modalities, such as art, music, words, and drawings together may heighten the impact of self-expression.

Cameron, Julia. *The Artist's Way: A Spiritual Path to Higher Creativity.* Los Angeles: Jeremy P. Tarcher, 1992.

This book has become a classic for people who want to spur their imagination and explore their creativity. Cameron offers a weekly step-by-step process for self-discovery that includes many journal exercises. She includes helpful descriptions of pitfalls and how to avoid them.

LANGUAGES OF HEALING

DeSalvo, Louise. *Writing As a Way of Healing: How Telling Our Stories Transforms Our Lives.* San Francisco: Harper San Francisco, 1999.

This book offers both a powerful introduction to the healing powers of writing and practical advice for getting started. The author draws on the works of literary figures and aspiring writers to show how physical and psychological wounds can be healed through writing that comes from a deep authentic place.

Goldberg, Natalie. *Writing Down the Bones: Freeing the Writer Within.* Boston: Shambhala, 1986.

A truly inspirational guide for aspiring and experienced writers alike, this book offers practical and down-to-earth advice that helps de-mystify the process of writing. It offers humorous encouragement combined with a respect for the power of language to help us heal.

ON KEEPING A JOURNAL

Cameron, Julia. *The Right to Write: An Invitation and Initiation into the Writing Life.* New York: Jeremy P. Tarcher/Putnam, 1998.

This book offers an intimate glimpse of one writer's struggles along with straightforward exercises to support the ongoing process of meeting oneself and the world through the practice of regular writing, whatever the form. The tone is conversational and inviting.

Rico, Gabriele Lusser. *Writing the Natural Way: Using Right-Brain Techniques to Release Your Expressive Powers.* Los Angeles: Jeremy Tarcher/Putnam, 1983.

A useful and usable book, full of ideas for stimulating the senses and mind of aspiring and experienced writers alike.

RECLAIMING THE ARTIST WITHIN

Ganim, Barbara. *Art and Healing: Using Expressive Art to Heal Your Body, Mind, and Spirit.* New York: Three Rivers Press, 1999.

Ganim offers a deep wealth of guided meditations coupled with creative techniques to connect the reader with inner feelings and to help express them through drawing. Chapters focus on healing the mind, healing the body, and healing the spirit.

Malchiodi, Cathy. *The Art Therapy Sourcebook*. Los Angeles: Lowell House, 1998.

With great clarity, this book covers the therapeutic value of artistic expressions as a way of knowing and communicating. It provides guidelines for creating and interpreting art and many useful exercises and examples. This is one of the best introductions to the field of art therapy.

Capacchione, Lucia. *The Picture of Health, Healing your Life Through Art*. Santa Monica: Hay House, 1990.

This book offers an approach to getting in touch with your "inner artist" and "inner healer" through the use of words and drawings. The author provides a wide variety of exercises that can be used to assist in thinking and feeling on paper. This is one of several helpful books she has written on the subject.

SOUND, MUSIC, AND HEALING

Campbell, Don G. *The Mozart Effect: Tapping the Power of Music to Heal the Body, Strengthen the Mind, and Unlock the Creative Spirit*. New York: Avon Books, 1997.

This is the book that made people aware of the tremendous potential that sound and music have to promote healing. Campbell includes research studies as well as many exercises that help create a more "harmonious life." He offers a chapter on specific ways music has been used in treatment for a variety of mental, physical, and spiritual conditions.

Lane, Deforia. *Music as Medicine: Deforia Lane's Life of Music, Healing, and Faith*. Grand Rapids, MI: Zondervan Publishing House, 1994.

Deforia was the first music therapist to receive a grant to study music's effects on cancer patients. This uplifting autobi-

ography tells of Deforia's own journey through cancer and how she used music for herself and as a way to instill joy and hope in people who are ill and hospitalized.

AWAKENING THROUGH MOVEMENT

Feldenkrais, Moshe. *Body and Mature Behavior: A Study of Anxiety, Sex, Gravitation, and Learning.* New York: International Universities Press, Inc., 1950.

An important resource that describes how the re-education of the body enhances emotional as well as physical health. The author looks at the correlations between physiology, psychology, gravity, and healing.

Artress, Lauren. *Walking a Sacred Path: Rediscovering the Labyrinth as a Spiritual Tool.* New York: Riverhead Books, 1995.

This book introduced readers to the use of inner pilgrimage to deepen awareness. Walking the labyrinth can facilitate healing cognitively, physically, and spiritually.

Halprin, Anna. *Moving Toward Life: Five Decades of Transformational Dance.* Hanover, NH: University Press of New England, 1995.

This is a stimulating resource which incorporates movement, ritual, theories of healing, and images to encourage hope and action to heal individuals, communities, and the planet.

RELATIONSHIP AND HEALING

Nhat Hanh, Thich. *Being Peace.* Berkeley, CA: Parallax Press, 1987.

One of Thich Nhat Hanh's best-known works, Being Peace *introduces the reader to a form of spiritual practice that has the potential to offer healing in the face of great suffering. The author's form of engaged Buddhism, which emerged out of his* experience as a peace activist during the war in Vietnam, is presented as a path for bringing peace into the world, starting within ourselves and then our communities.

CONNECTING WITH OUR INNERSELVES

Schwartz, Richard. *Internal Family Systems Therapy*. New York: Guilford Press, 1994.

This book gives a theoretical and practical introduction to internal family systems therapy, in which helpful examples illustrating the relationships between "parts" and "self" are offered. It would be most useful to therapists who are interested in applying the internal systems concepts and methods to their own practice.

Satir, Virginia. *Your Many Faces*. Berkeley, CA: Celestial Arts, 1998.

This is a readable and accessible presentation of different aspects of individual's inner system. Satir approaches the task as one of getting to know the cast of characters each of us brings to the "stage production" of our lives.

Rogers, Carl. *A Way of Being*. New York: Houghton Mifflin, 1980.

Carl Rogers summarizes what he sees as the central contributions of his life work. He gives clear expression to his insight that the most important aspect of helping others is the way we are in relationship to ourselves and to the person we are trying to assist. Our ability to help is not the result of technique but derives from our way of being.

HONORING OTHERS

Levine, S., and Levine, O. *Embracing the Beloved*. New York: Doubleday, 1995.

This book applies a mindfulness perspective to intimate relationships. It offers fifty-one short chapters on spirituality in relationships, along with numerous meditations for individuals and dyads.

Welwood, John. *Journey of the Heart: Intimate Relationship and the Path of Love.* New York: Harper Collins, 1990.

This book describes the process of embracing one's intimate relationships as a spiritual practice and path. It discusses such topics as falling in love, commitment, and the sacredness of marriage.

Whitmyer, Claude, ed. *In the Company of Others: Making Community in the Modern World.* New York: Jeremy P. Tarcher Perigree, 1993.

This book offers chapters by a variety of authors on topics such as seeking community, making community, and living community. It includes many examples of the importance of people coming together, and different forms that community can take.

THE WAY OF WORK

Welwood, John, ed. *Ordinary Magic: Everyday Life as Spiritual Path.* Boston: Shambhala, 1992.

A classic collection of writings by writers from varied contemplative traditions addressing the question of integrating spiritual practice with life in the world of work, family, and community.

Dass, Ram, and Gorman, Paul. *How Can I Help? Stories and Reflections on Service.* New York: Knopf, 1985.

This book is a straight-talking introduction to finding and sustaining an authentic connection with one's work.

Elgin, Duane. *Voluntary Simplicity: Toward a Way of Life*

That is Outwardly Simple, Inwardly Rich. Rev. ed. New York: William Morrow/Quill, 1993.

A highly regarded introduction to learning how to live more simply in an increasingly complex world. Included is a questionnaire to help readers better assess their own needs.

FRUITS OF THE HARVEST: COMPASSION

The Dalai Lama and Cutler, Howard C. *The Art of Happiness. A Handbook for Living.* New York: Riverhead Books, 1998.

This book is a simple but not simplistic depiction of the fruits of the spiritual path. While the emphasis is on Buddhism, the authors' advice applies to individuals from all traditions.

COMING HOME TO SIMPLICITY

Kornfield, Jack. *After the Ecstasy, the Laundry: How the Heart Grows Wise on the Spiritual Path.* New York: Bantam Books, 2000.

This book is a helpful guide for individuals on how to translate spiritual insights into their everyday lives and relationships. Through stories from the lives of ordinary individuals as well as the wisdom traditions, Jack Kornfield brings a deep understanding based on spiritual practice and how to integrate a sense of the sacred into ordinary activities.

Contributors

MOLLY VASS-LEHMAN was a faculty member in the Graduate Program in Holistic Health Care at Western Michigan University for 20 years. She was director of the program from 1985 to 1998. In addition to her University appointment, she has served as a consultant to and founding fellow of the Fetzer Institute, an organization dedicated to furthering research and education in mind-body health and medicine. Molly is a nationally-recognized speaker on the impact of the field of holistic health on such areas as counseling, psychology, and education. For the past twenty years she has also maintained a private counseling practice for individuals and organizations. Her research and publications focus on the areas of health promotion, holistic health, and human relationships. With extensive ties to Christian monastic traditions and an ongoing interest in contemplative practices from all faiths, Molly and her husband established a non-profit interfaith retreat center known as GilChrist. They continue to serve on its board of advisors.

PAULA W. JAMISON is a faculty member in the Occupational Therapy Department at Western Michigan University and also teaches in the Graduate Program in Holistic Health Care. She received her Ph.D. from the University of Chicago in French literature and worked in the fields of publishing and human services before returning to

WMU to obtain a Master's degree in Occupational Therapy and a Graduate Certificate in Holistic Health Care. A meditation instructor for the past ten years, Paula has been exploring the impact of language and contemplative practice on the healing process and the role of the clinician. She has translated and edited books in the fields of anthropology and history of religions and is co-producer, with her husband, of a series of videotapes documenting Tibetan culture in exile and contemporary Asian and North American Buddhist teachers. In addition to her sitting meditation practice, she has been a consistent journal keeper since 1982 and teaches Holistic Approaches to Healing through Writing and Story for the Holistic Health Program.

 **THOMAS HOLMES** directed the Holistic Health Care Program at Western Michigan University from 1998-2002, and is currently a faculty member. He received his Ph.D. in Counseling Psychology from Michigan State University and also holds Masters' degrees in Clinical Psychology and Social Work. He taught in the School of Social Work at WMU from 1985 to 1996, when he joined the Holistic Health Care Program faculty. He has practiced as a psychotherapist and has trained psychotherapists at the graduate and post-graduate level since 1985. His publications focus on such topics as the evaluation of psychotherapy, international issues in mental health, and the integration of spirituality and psychotherapy. He has specialized in the study of the relationship between spirituality, psychotherapy, health, and healing. In addition to his background in psychotherapy, Tom has been practicing and studying in the universalist spiritual tradition and has also studied with exiled Vietnamese Buddhist master Thich Nhat Hanh. These combined

areas of interest have led Tom increasingly to study how our biological, psychological, social, and spiritual systems interrelate, and how our most effective healing and prevention interventions incorporate as many levels of the system as possible.

 **GAYL WALKER** is a faculty member in the Graduate Program in Holistic Health Care at Western Michigan University. She is also an art therapist, artist, and graphic designer. She holds a Master's degree in Holistic Art Therapy from Antioch University, a BFA from Michigan State University, and a Graduate Certificate in Holistic Health Care from Western Michigan University. The courses she teaches focus on the healing potential of the expressive arts, including the visual arts, music, drama, poetry, and movement. She also is on the faculty of the Kalamazoo Institute of Arts. As director and co-founder of Chrysalis Community, Cancer Help Program she offers holistic retreats and workshops to enhance the quality of life for people with cancer. "Addicted" to making art, Gay continues to explore her own creativity using a variety of media. She is the creator of numerous exhibits featuring her work and the art of individuals affected by cancer and illness. These have traveled to hospitals and cancer centers for ten years. She also created and manages the Diane's Way Expressive Arts Program for Borgess Visiting Nurse and Hospice, which bring a variety of expressive arts into the homes of hospice patients. Using her rich background in graphic design and love of photography, Gay designed this book.

KAREN HORNEFFER received her Ph.D. in Clinical and Community Psychology from the University of Illinois. Her interests have focused on the area of health psychology and the pursuit of healing modalities that bridge mind, body, and spirit. She has worked on the field of medical education teaching physicians about holistic approaches to health care. She currently is the Director of the Graduate Program in Holistic Health Care at Western Michigan University and has a private practice as a psychotherapist.

BARBARA TOSHALIS teaches others how to access wisdom, power, and joy through movement, whether structured or spontaneous. She holds Masters' degrees in Physical Therapy and Social Work and serves as a spiritual director. She facilitates movement within groups, classes, or during individual sessions of spiritual direction or psychotherapy. She also has taken special training in Creative and Authentic Movement. Her vision is to reintroduce movement to North Americans as a source of healing and inspiration.

The following people shared personal odysseys with us:

K'ANNA BURTON received her Master's degree in Education from Michigan State University, a Graduate Certificate in Holistic Health Care from Western Michigan University, and has over twenty years of diverse teaching/facilitating experience. Her background in holistic health care, earth education, and community group building blends holistic perspectives in a heart-centered learning environment. Inspiriting the workplace culture has been an on-going passion for K'Anna through her work as co-founder of Grace Institute. A believer in lifelong learning, K'Anna continues to explore lifestyle choices that honor the unfolding of the body, mind, and spirit within self and with others.

FRITZ MACDONALD received his Ph.D. from the University of Tennessee College of Social Work. His wife, Linda, is an ordained minister for the Presbyterian Church USA. His sons

Wade, Jaymes, and Alec have taught him much about loving kindness and forgiveness. Fritz is Associate Professor in the School of Social Work at Western Michigan University. He is Managing Editor of the *Journal of Sociology and Social Welfare*.

DIANE MELVIN received her B.A. from the University of Minnesota in American Studies, and her M.A. from the University of Illinois in Environmental Studies. She worked at the Kalamazoo Nature Center as an environmental educator, and has taught classes at Western Michigan University (in Environmental Studies) and Kalamazoo Valley Community College (on the topics of Political Science, Women's History, Ecology, and College Writing). She is passionate in her pursuits to heal our society and planet.

Permissions

Grateful acknowledgment is made to the following publishers and authors for permission to reprint material from their books.

From *Zorba the Greek* by Nikos Kazantzakis . Copyright 1953 and renewed 1981, by Simon and Schuster. Used by permission of Beacon Press.

From *A Path With Heart* by Jack Kornfield. Copyright 1993 by Jack Kornfield. Used by permission of The Bantam Dell Publishing Group.

From *Sleeping with Bread* by Dennis Linn, Sheila Fabricant Linn, and Matthew Linn. Used by permission of Paulist Press.

From *A Waterfall of Hands* (in manuscript) by Mark Nepo. Used by permission of the author.

From "Passing Angels: The Arts of Spiritual Discernment" by Wendy Wright. Used by permission of *Weavings*, Vol. X, No. 6 (November/December 1995)

From *New and Selected Poems by Mary Oliver*. Copyright 1992 by Mary Oliver. Used by permission of Beacon Press.

David Whyte. "Easter Morning in Wales," from *Where Many Rivers Meet*. Langley, WA: Many Rivers Press, 1990. (Copyright held by David Whyte, not by Many Rivers Press.)

Photographers

We extend our gratitude to the following photographers whose inspiring visions have complemented the text. They have graciously granted permission to share their work.

Lewis Batts, Kalamazoo, Michigan
pages xv, 15, 24, 55, 72, 99, 133, 153, 191

Mary Decker, South Haven, Michigan
page 195

Diane Hill, Coralville, Iowa
pages vii, 75

John Howie, Three Rivers, Michigan
page 53

Barbara Jeska, Plainwell, Michigan
pages xi, 3, 19, 103, 175

David Kamm, Kalamazoo, Michigan
pages 27, 79, 81, 83, 125, 137

David Lubbers, Grand Rapids, Michigan
pages 1, 9, 11, 37, 47, 49, 109, 119, 143, 167, 181, 207

Amie Mack, Oceanside, CA
pages 33, 171, 205

Sally Putney, Richland, Michigan
pages 13, 43, 45, 117, 123, 131, 203

Gay Walker, Richland, Michigan
pages 106, 185, 199

John Walker, Richland, Michigan
pages iii, 4, 173, 233

Mary Whalen, Kalamazoo, Michigan
pages 63, 140, 159, 163

Pam Wilson
pages 7, 183, 201

For more information on the Graduate Holistic Health Care
Certificate Program at Western Michigan University contact:

Holistic Health Care Certificate Program

Western Michigan University

1903 West Michigan Avenue

Kalamazoo, Michigan 49008-5212

Phone: 269-387-2650 or 269-387-3556

Fax: 269-387-3348

e-mail: holistic-info@wmich.edu

web: www.wmich.edu/hhs/holistichealth